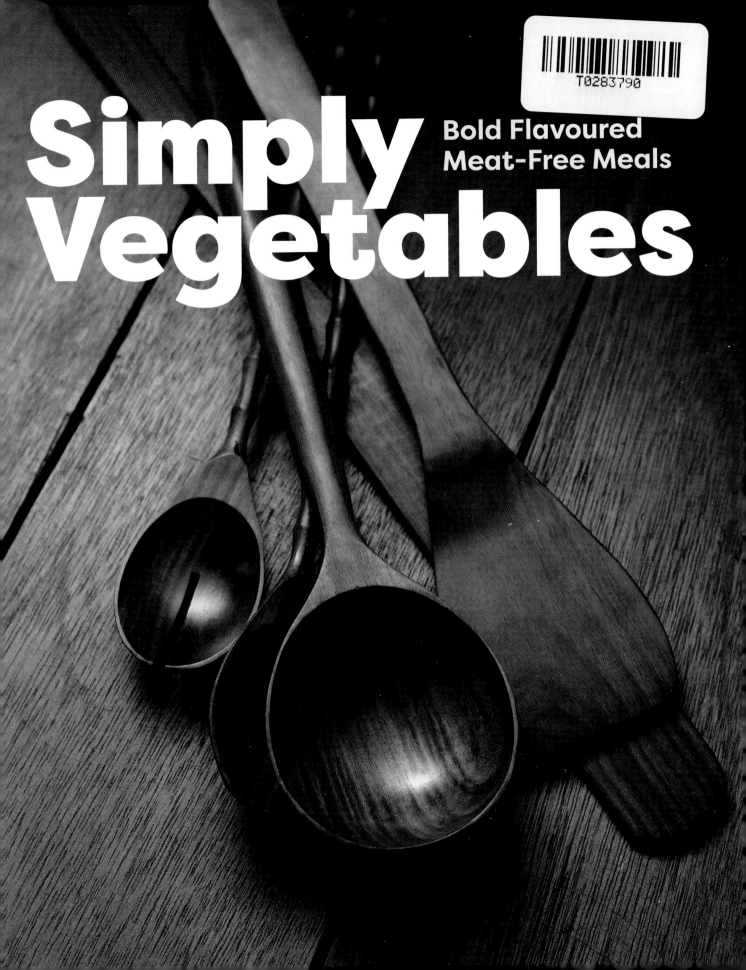

Simply Vegetables

Bold Flavoured Meat-Free Meals

The Publisher wishes to thank Metrojaya Berhad, Malaysia for the loan of their crockery and utensils and Li-Ter, Malaysia for sponsoring the vegetarian food supplies.

Chef's Assistant: Margaret Wong
Photographer: Jenhor Siow

First published 2003 as CCC: Vegetarian Feasts and 2009 as Asian Vegetarian Feasts
This new edition 2023

Published by Marshall Cavendish Cuisine
An imprint of Marshall Cavendish International

A member of the
Times Publishing Group

Other Marshall Cavendish Offices:
Marshall Cavendish Corporation, 800 Westchester Ave, Suite N-641, Rye Brook, NY 10573, USA
• Marshall Cavendish International (Thailand) Co Ltd, 253 Asoke, 16th Floor, Sukhumvit 21 Road, Klongtoey Nua, Wattana, Bangkok 10110, Thailand • Marshall Cavendish (Malaysia) Sdn Bhd, Times Subang, Lot 46, Subang Hi-Tech Industrial Park, Batu Tiga, 40000 Shah Alam, Selangor Darul Ehsan, Malaysia

Printed in Singapore

Simply Vegetables

Bold Flavoured Meat-Free Meals

Azrah Kamala Shashi

mc Marshall Cavendish
Cuisine

Azrah Kamala Shashi is a professionally trained chef with more than 30 years of cooking and teaching experience. She has won accolades for her cooking skills, bagged gold medals and prizes in cooking competitions and received honorary certificates from the food and beverage industry. As a teacher, food stylist and culinary consultant, Azrah is also an expert in Indian, Malay, Filipino, Indonesian, Thai and Turkish cuisines. She was invited by organisations such as Nestle, PELITAWANIS and BAKTI to judge cooking competitions.

The multilingual Azrah has appeared on Malaysian television programmes of various languages, including *Kesuma, Nona, Mawar, Citarasa in Malay, Good Morning Malaysia* in English, *Magalir Neram* in Tamil and *Mei Sek Theen Tay* in Cantonese. She also contributes recipes to English and Malay newspapers and magazines, including *New Straits Times, Malay Mail, Her World, Utusan Melayu, Berita Harian* and *Nona*. She is also a popular guest speaker on Malay, English and Tamil radio shows.

For my dearest husband, S. Shashitharan

Preface

Malay

Chinese

"Nothing will benefit human health and increase chances of survival of life on Earth as much as the evolution to a vegetarian diet."

Albert Einstein

Vegetarianism is becoming more widespread today. The reasons behind this include health consciousness, spiritual and ecological awareness and a love for animals.

There are vegans, those who exclude all foods of animal origin from their diet, lacto-vegetarians, those who exclude all animal flesh and eggs but consume milk, ovo-vegetarians, those who exclude all animal flesh and milk but consume eggs, ovo-lacto vegetarian, those who exclude all animal flesh but consume milk and eggs and pesco-vegetarians, those who avoid meat and poultry but consume fish and seafood. The recipes found in this book are vegetable and soy-based and will cater to these groups at varying degrees.

Non-vegetarians, however, will also benefit from the recipes found here. A vegetable-based diet is more likely to meet current dietary recommendations for the percentage of fat, carbohydrates and proteins than an omnivorous diet. There is also evidence that such a diet reduces the risk of chronic degenerative diseases like diabetes mellitus, hypertension, cancer and heart disease, while reducing blood cholesterol levels and incidences of diverticulitis and piles.

Despite these obvious benefits, people still shy away from vegetarian fare as they perceive that it is bland and boring, but nothing can be further from the truth! If vegetarian food is well cooked and presented, you will never miss eating meat or poultry.

The availability of mock meat and seafood is also a great boon to those 'die-hard' meat eaters. Since taste is not solely dependent on the taste buds, the texture and look of these mock items help the visual senses forget that they are of soy origin.

In this book, the recipes are nutritious and easy-to-follow. I have also developed the recipes with Malay, Indian, Chinese, Thai and Western flavours to help you vary your menu.

As you try these recipes, you will find that cooking vegetarian meals can be fun, and with the added bonus that you are dishing out healthy food, your adventure in the kitchen will be doubly satisfying.

Happy cooking!

AZRAH KAMALA SHASHI

Dumplings and Vegetables
in Coconut Milk Soup

ACAR BUAH-BUAHAN MALAYSIA (PICKLED FRUITS)

• PREPARATION TIME: 45 MIN • COOKING TIME: 25 MIN • SERVES 8

INGREDIENTS

Dried chillies	15, softened in hot water and drained
Fennel seeds	1 Tbsp
Cumin seeds	2 Tbsp
Coriander (cilantro) leaves	1 sprig
Cooking oil	180 ml
Shallots	10, each cut in half
Garlic	10 cloves, each cut in half
Mustard seeds	1 tsp
Sesame seeds	2 Tbsp
Water	125 ml
Vinegar	375 ml
Sugar	125 g
Prunes	150 g
Preserved nutmeg	150 g, cut into 1-cm pieces
Sultanas	100 g
Preserved plum	150 g
Pickled mustard stem	150 g, cut into 1-cm pieces
Bird's eye chillies	10
Red chillies	5
Green chillies	5

METHOD

• Fry dried chillies, fennel seeds, cumin seeds and coriander leaves in a dry wok until lightly fragrant. Let cool, then grind together until fine. Set aside.

• Heat oil in a wok and fry shallots, garlic, mustard seeds and sesame seeds until brown. Add ground ingredients and fry until aromatic. Oil will start to emerge.

• Add water, vinegar, sugar and bring to the boil. Add prunes, preserved nutmeg, sultanas, preserved plum, pickled mustard stem, bird's eye chillies, red and green chillies and cook for 25 minutes.

• Let cool before bottling. Serve as a side dish to complement curry and rice dishes.

CHEF'S NOTE

These pickles are ideal served with *nasi briyani* or *nasi minyak*.

NASI MINYAK LOBAK MERAH (CARROT FRIED RICE)

• PREPARATION TIME: 30 MIN • COOKING TIME: 25 MIN • SERVES 6

INGREDIENTS

Ghee (clarified butter)	125 g
Big onions	2, sliced
Garlic	2 cloves, sliced thinly
Cloves	4
Cinnamon	3.5-cm length
Cardamom	4 pods
White peppercorns	6
Pandan (screwpine) leaves	2-3, tied into a knot
Long-grain rice	500 g
Evaporated milk	125 ml
Carrot	200 g, cut into cubes
Sultanas	125 g
Salt to taste	
Water	625 ml
Red chilli	1, chopped
Fried onions	100 g
Cashew nuts	100 g, roasted

METHOD

• Heat ghee in a rice cooker and fry sliced onions, garlic, cloves, cinnamon, cardamom, peppercorns and pandan leaves until onions are light brown.

• Add rice and evaporated milk. Stir well.

• Add carrots, sultanas, salt and water. Leave rice to cook.

• Dish out and garnish with chopped chilli, fried onions and roasted cashew nuts before serving.

From top: Acar Buah-Buahan Malaysia (Pickled Fruits), Nasi Minyak Lobak Merah (Carrot Fried Rice)

GULAI SAYUR MASIN DENGAN NENAS (VEGETABLE PINEAPPLE CURRY)
• PREPARATION TIME: 25 MIN • COOKING TIME: 20 MIN • SERVES 6

INGREDIENTS

Salted vegetable	125 g, cut into 0.5-cm lengths
Pineapple	1
Shallots	6
Garlic	2 cloves
Fresh turmeric	2.5-cm knob
Dried chillies	10
Thick coconut milk	125 ml (refer to page 82)
Thin coconut milk	750 ml (refer to page 82)
Dried sour fruit slices (asam gelugur)	2
Salt to taste	

METHOD

• Rinse salted vegetable and soak in water for 30 minutes. Squeeze out water and set aside.

• Clean, core and cut pineapple into rings and then cut each ring in half. Set aside.

• Combine shallots, garlic, turmeric and dried chillies and grind finely together.

• Pour thin coconut milk into a pot and add ground ingredients. Mix well and bring to the boil, stirring constantly.

• Add salted vegetable, pineapple, dried sour fruit slices and salt to taste. Return to the boil for 5 minutes. Stir mixture continuously so coconut milk does not coagulate. Add thick coconut milk and stir well.

• Serve hot with rice.

NASI REMPAH KACANG KUDA (SPICED RICE WITH CHICKPEAS)
• PREPARATION TIME: 25 MIN • COOKING TIME: 30 MIN • SERVES 6

INGREDIENTS

Chickpeas	250 g, soaked for 6 hours
Basmati rice	500 g
Turmeric powder	1 tsp
Cumin seeds	1 tsp
Lemongrass (serai)	2 stalks, cut into small pieces
Ginger	1-cm knob
Garlic	3 cloves
Shallots	5
Ghee or oil	125 g
Water	500 ml
Thick coconut milk	250 ml
Salt to taste	
Fried onions	100 g
Coriander (cilantro) leaves	2 sprigs, cut into short lengths

METHOD

• Pressure-cook or boil chickpeas until almost tender. Set aside.

• Rinse rice, drain and set aside.

• Combine turmeric powder, cumin seeds, lemongrass, ginger, garlic and shallots and grind until fine.

• Heat ghee or oil in a rice cooker. Add ground ingredients and fry until aromatic.

• Add water, rice, coconut milk, chickpeas and salt to taste. Leave rice to cook.

• Dish out and garnish with fried onions and coriander leaves before serving.

From top: Gulai Sayur Masin Dengan Nenas (Vegetable Pineapple Curry), Nasi Rempah Kacang Kuda (Spiced Rice with Chickpeas)

KENTANG DENGAN SAYURAN BERBUNGKUS DAUN PANDAN (PANDAN LEAF VEGETABLE PARCELS)

• PREPARATION TIME: 25 MIN • COOKING TIME: 30 MIN • SERVES 6

INGREDIENTS

Vegetarian mock chicken	100 g, cut into 1.5-cm cubes and fried
Potatoes	2, big, boiled and mashed
Water chestnuts	6, cut into 0.5-cm cubes
Frozen mixed vegetables	200 g
Coriander (cilantro) leaves	1 stalk, cut into 0.5-cm lengths
Eggs	2, lightly beaten
Salt	1 tsp
Fried onions	50 g
Garlic	2 cloves, chopped finely
Ground white pepper	1 tsp
Cooking oil	500 ml
Pandan (screwpine) leaves	15

METHOD

• Combine all ingredients except pandan leaves and mix well.

• Take a spoonful of combined ingredients and place on a pandan leaf. Fold into a triangular shape and secure with a toothpick. Repeat until ingredients are used up.

• Heat oil in a wok and deep-fry pandan leaf parcels until leaves turn dark green. Drain excess oil and serve.

CHEF'S NOTE

The eggs in this recipe may be substituted with breadcrumbs.

KERABU BETIK MUDA (YOUNG PAPAYA SALAD)

• PREPARATION TIME: 30 MIN • SERVES 4

INGREDIENTS

Young papaya	500 g
Red chilli	1
Bird's eye chillies	5
Shallots	6
Lime juice	extracted from 1 lime
Fried grated coconut (*kerisik*)	1½ Tbsp
Sugar	1 Tbsp
Salt	1 tsp

METHOD

• Slice off papaya skin and cut papaya into slices. Set aside.

• Pound red chilli, bird's eye chillies and shallots roughly. Mix in lime juice, fried coconut, sugar and salt to taste.

• Add to sliced papaya and mix well. Serve.

From top: Kerabu Betik Muda (Young Papaya Salad), Kentang Dengan Sayuran Berbungkus Daun Pandan (Pandan Leaf Vegetable Parcels)

LEMAK SAYUR MANIS CILI API (VEGETABLE COCONUT CURRY)

• PREPARATION TIME: 30 MIN • COOKING TIME: 25 MIN • SERVES 4

INGREDIENTS

Sayur manis	300 g
Bird's eye chillies	10
Fresh turmeric	1.5-cm knob
Shallots	6
Thin coconut milk	1 litre (*refer to page 82*)
Lemongrass (*serai*)	2 stalks, bruised
Salt to taste	
Thick coconut milk	125 ml (*refer to page 82*)

METHOD

• Clean and wash *sayur manis*. Drain and set aside.

• Grind bird's eye chillies, turmeric and shallots finely together.

• In a pot, combine thin coconut milk, lemongrass and ground ingredients. Bring to the boil.

• Add *sayur manis* and salt to taste. Leave to simmer for 5 minutes.

• Add thick coconut milk and stir well. Leave to cook for another 2 minutes.

• Dish out and serve hot with rice.

CHEF'S NOTE

There is no English name for *sayur manis*. The tender variety of this vegetable is called Sabah vegetables.

KERABU JANTUNG PISANG (BANANA FLOWER SALAD)

• PREPARATION TIME: 35 MIN • COOKING TIME: 20 MIN • SERVES 4

INGREDIENTS

Banana flower	1
Water	500 ml
Thick coconut milk	250 ml (*refer to page 82*)
Big onions	2, sliced into rings
Fried grated coconut (*kerisik*)	125 g
Red chillies	4
Garlic	2 cloves
Lime juice	extracted from 2 limes
Salt to taste	
Sugar	2 Tbsp
Red chilli	1, chopped

METHOD

• Clean and cut banana flower finely. Boil for 5 minutes until tender and drain.

• Place boiled banana flower in a bowl and mix well with coconut milk. Pour into a wok and heat for 2–3 minutes.

• Grind onions, fried grated coconut, red chillies and garlic roughly together. Add to wok and stir.

• Season with lime juice, salt and sugar. Toss well.

• Garnish with chopped chillies and serve with rice.

CHEF'S NOTE

Use only the young banana flower. If using more mature flowers, use the inner shoot.

From top: Lemak Sayur Manis Cili Api (Vegetable Coconut Curry), Kerabu Jantung Pisang (Banana Flower Salad)

SAYUR RAMPAI SARI MALAYSIA (MALAYSIAN MIXED VEGETABLES)

· PREPARATION TIME: 35 MIN · COOKING TIME: 30 MIN · SERVES 6

INGREDIENTS

Cooking oil	500 ml
Fermented soy bean cake (tempeh)	400 g
Firm bean curd	2 pieces, sliced into 1.5-cm lengths
Red chillies	4, 2 sliced and 2 whole
Garlic	2 cloves
Shallots	6
Ginger	2.5-cm knob
Big onions	2, sliced into rings
Long beans	250 g, cut into 2.5-cm lengths
Glass noodles	150 g, soaked for 5 minutes
Cabbage	150 g, shredded
Bean curd sheet	1, soaked and torn in pieces
Thick coconut milk	125 ml (refer to page 82)
Salt to taste	

METHOD

· Heat oil in a wok and fry fermented soy bean cake until brown. Drain and set aside.

· Using the same wok, fry bean curd pieces until brown. Drain and set aside.

· Grind 2 whole red chillies, garlic, shallots and ginger together until fine.

· Using the same wok, remove all but 3 Tbsp oil and fry ground ingredients until fragrant. Add sliced onions, long beans, glass noodles, cabbage, bean curd sheet, fried bean curd pieces and fermented soy bean cake and stir well.

· Add coconut milk, salt and sliced red chillies and stir well. Cook until dry.

· Serve hot with rice.

NASI KABILI (KABILI RICE)

· PREPARATION TIME: 30 MIN · COOKING TIME: 25 MIN · SERVES 6

INGREDIENTS

Basmati rice	500 g
Fried onions	3 Tbsp
Sultanas	30 g
Coriander (cilantro) leaves	1 tsp
Fennel seeds	1 tsp
Cumin seeds	1 tsp
White peppercorns	2 tsp
Ginger	2.5-cm knob
Big onions	3; 1 chopped, 2 sliced thinly
Ghee (clarified butter)	60 g
Cloves	4
Cinnamon	3.5-cm length
Cardamom	4 pods
Thin coconut milk	750 ml (refer to page 82)
Salt to taste	
Cashew nuts	1 Tbsp, roasted
Coriander leaves	1 sprig, chopped

METHOD

· Rinse rice, drain and set aside.

· Grind fried onions, coriander leaves, fennel seeds, cumin seeds, white peppercorns, ginger and chopped onion together until fine. Set aside.

· Heat ghee in a rice cooker and fry sliced onions, cloves, cinnamon and cardamom until aromatic and the onions are brown.

· Add ground ingredients and fry until oil rises to the top. Add coconut milk and bring to the boil.

· Add Basmati rice to the boiling mixture and salt to taste. Close rice cooker and leave to cook until rice is done.

· Garnish cooked rice with cashew nuts and coriander leaves before serving.

CHEF'S NOTE

You may also top the rice with egg strips or sultanas if desired.

From top: Sayur Rampai Sari Malaysia (Malaysian Mixed Vegetables), Nasi Kabili (Kabili Rice)

KERABU TAUGE
(BEAN SPROUTS SALAD)
• PREPARATION TIME: 30 MIN • SERVES 4

INGREDIENTS

Bean sprouts	200 g, blanched
Cabbage	200 g, shredded
Lime juice	1 Tbsp
Torch ginger flower	1, sliced finely
Coriander (cilantro) leaves	30 g, cut into 0.5-cm lengths
Red chilli	1, sliced finely
Fried grated coconut (*kerisik*)	50 g
Salt and sugar to taste	

METHOD

• Toss ingredients together in a bowl and mix well. Transfer to a salad bowl and serve cold.

CURRY LAKSA
• PREPARATION TIME: 30 MIN • COOKING TIME: 35 MIN • SERVES 6

INGREDIENTS

Cooking oil	3 Tbsp
Vegetarian curry paste	250 g (*refer to page 82*)
Thin coconut milk	2.5 litres (*refer to page 82*)
Curry leaves	4 sprigs
Cream of mushroom soup	125 ml
Lemongrass (*serai*)	4 stalks
Fried bean curd puffs	100 g, each cut in half
Sugar	2 Tbsp
Salt to taste	
Yellow noodles	1 kg, scalded in hot water

GARNISHING

Cucumber	250 g, shredded
Pineapple	250 g, shredded
Bean sprouts	125 g, blanched
Potato	1, boiled and cut into 2.5-cm cubes

METHOD

• Heat oil in a non-stick pan and fry curry paste until aromatic and oil surfaces. Set aside.

• In a stockpot, combine coconut milk, curry paste, curry leaves, cream of mushroom soup, lemongrass and fried bean curd puffs. Bring to the boil.

• Add sugar and salt to taste. Lower heat to a simmer.

• To serve, place some yellow noodles in a serving bowl and top with shredded cucumber, shredded pineapple, bean sprouts and potatoes. Ladle some soup over and serve hot.

From top: Kerabu Tauge (Bean Sprouts Salad), Curry Laksa

SERUNDING KACANG MERAH DAN KACANG KUDA (KIDNEY BEAN AND CHICKPEA SALAD)

• PREPARATION TIME: 30 MIN • COOKING TIME: 30 MIN • SERVES 6

INGREDIENTS

Turmeric powder	1/2 tsp
Coriander (cilantro) leaves	2 sprigs
Shallots	6
Garlic	4 cloves
Salt	1 tsp
Cumin seeds	1 tsp
Ginger	1.5-cm knob
Lemongrass (serai)	1 stalk
Tamarind pulp	1 tsp
Cooking oil	4 Tbsp
Water	125 ml
Sugar	1 Tbsp
Light soy sauce	1 tsp
Fried ground coconut (kerisik)	150 g
Red kidney beans	250 g, boiled
Chickpeas	250 g, boiled
Tamarind juice	1 Tbsp

METHOD

• Grind turmeric powder, coriander leaves, shallots, garlic, salt, cumin seeds, ginger, lemongrass and tamarind pulp together until fine.

• Heat oil in a wok and fry ground ingredients until aromatic. Add water, sugar, light soy sauce and salt and stir well. Cook for 3 minutes.

• Add fried grated coconut, kidney beans, chickpeas and tamarind juice and stir well. Cook until dry.

• Dish out and serve hot.

MAMAK MEE (INDIAN FRIED NOODLES)

• PREPARATION TIME: 20 MIN • COOKING TIME: 20 MIN • SERVES 3

INGREDIENTS

Firm yellow bean curd	3 pieces, cut into 0.25-cm slices
Salt	as needed
Cooking oil	
Big onions	2, sliced
Tomatoes	1, sliced
Cabbage	50 g, shredded
Flowering cabbage (choy sum)	100 g, cut into 3-cm lengths
Chilli paste	1 Tbsp
Chilli sauce	4 Tbsp
Dark soy sauce	1 Tbsp
Light soy sauce	3 Tbsp
Yellow egg noodles	400 g
Eggs	2, lightly beaten
Bean sprouts	200 g
Red chilli	1, sliced
Green chilli	1, sliced

METHOD

• Sprinkle some salt over bean curd pieces.

• Heat oil in a wok and deep-fry bean curd until brown. Drain and set aside.

• Leave 2 Tbsp oil in the wok and sauté onions until soft. Add tomatoes, cabbage and flowering cabbage and stir-fry for 2-3 minutes.

• Add chilli paste, chilli sauce, soy sauces and 1 tsp salt. Stir well to mix. Add noodles and toss well.

• Push noodles to one side of wok. Add 1 Tbsp oil and pour in beaten egg. Spoon noodles over egg and let it cook for 1 minute before stir-frying to mix.

• Add bean sprouts and red and green chillies. Stir-fry to mix. Dish out and serve hot.

From top: Serunding Kacang Merah dan Kacang Kuda (Kidney Beans and Chickpeas Salad), Mamak Mee (Indian Fried Noodles)

DUMPLING SOUP

• PREPARATION TIME: 30 MIN • COOKING TIME 25 MIN • SERVES 4

INGREDIENTS

FILLING

Dried Chinese mushrooms	50 g, softened and cut into 0.5-cm cubes
Water chestnuts	50 g, cut into 0.5-cm cubes
Mixed vegetables	50 g
Vegetarian minced prawns	50 g, soaked and squeezed of excess water
Coriander (cilantro) leaves	1 stalk, cut into 0.5-cm lengths
Sugar	1/2 tsp
Salt	1/2 tsp
Light soy sauce	1 tsp
Cornflour	1 Tbsp, mixed with 1 Tbsp water

DUMPLINGS

Wonton skin	20 pieces
Vegetable stock	1.25 litres (refer to page 82)
Bean sprouts	70 g
Chives	70 g, cut into 1.5-cm lengths
Salt to taste	

METHOD

• Heat some oil in a wok and stir-fry all the filling ingredients for 2 minutes. Thicken with cornstarch, cool and set aside.

• To make dumplings, put 1 Tbsp filling on a wonton skin. Bring the edges together and seal with a little flour and water mixture. Continue until all the ingredients are used up. Keep dumplings aside.

• Bring vegetable stock to the boil. Add bean sprouts, chives and salt to taste.

• Lower dumplings into the stock and let it return to the boil. Cook for 5 minutes or until dumplings float. Serve hot.

CHEF'S NOTE

To save time on preparation, the vegetable stock can also be made using vegetable stock cubes.

BLACK PEPPER MOCK CHICKEN DRUMSTICKS

• PREPARATION TIME: 30 MIN • COOKING TIME: 25 MIN • SERVES 6

INGREDIENTS

Mock chicken drumsticks	8 pieces
Sesame seeds	30 g
Cornflour	125 g
Cooking oil for deep-frying	1 litre

MARINADE

Freshly ground black pepper	1 1/2 Tbsp
Light soy sauce	1 1/2 Tbsp
Vegetarian oyster sauce	2 Tbsp
Salt	1 tsp
Sugar	1 Tbsp

VEGETABLES

Big onion	50 g, cut into strips
Celery	50 g, cut into strips
Spring onions (scallions)	50 g, cut into strips
Green capsicums (bell peppers)	50 g, cored and cut into strips
Red chilli	1, cut into strips
Carrot	100 g, cut into strips

SAUCE

Honey	1 1/2 Tbsp
Lemon juice	50 ml
Worcester sauce	1 1/2 Tbsp
Sugar	2 Tbsp
Chilli sauce	2 Tbsp

METHOD

• Combine marinade ingredients and place mock chicken in to marinate for 1 hour.

• Heat oil for deep-frying in a wok.

• Coat marinated mock chicken with sesame seeds and cornflour, then deep-fry until golden brown over a slow fire. Drain well and set aside.

• Leave 2 Tbsp oil in the wok and stir-fry vegetables for 2 minutes.

• Combine sauce ingredients and add to the wok. Stir well. Allow sauce to boil until it thickens. Return fried mock chicken drumsticks to the wok and mix well.

• Dish out and serve hot.

From top: Dumpling Soup, Black Pepper Mock Chicken Drumsticks

KONG POH MIXED VEGETABLES (SPICY MIXED VEGETABLES)

• PREPARATION TIME: 30 MIN • COOKING TIME: 25 MIN • SERVES 4

INGREDIENTS

Cooking oil	3 Tbsp
Dried chillies	12, cut into 2.5-cm lengths
Ginger	2.5-cm knob, sliced
Garlic	2 cloves, chopped
Cauliflower	250 g, cut into florets
Red and green capsicums (bell peppers)	60 g each, cored and cut into 2.5-cm cubes
French beans	100 g, cut into 2.5-cm cubes
Chestnuts	100 g, cut into 2.5-cm cubes
Cashew nuts	150 g, toasted

SEASONING

Light soy sauce	1 1/2 Tbsp
Dark soy sauce	1 tsp
Sugar	1 Tbsp
Sesame oil	2 tsp
Cornflour	1 Tbsp
Vegetarian oyster sauce	2 Tbsp

METHOD

• Heat oil in a wok and fry dried chillies until brown. Dish out and set aside.

• In the same oil, fry ginger and garlic until light brown.

• Add all the vegetables and stir-fry for 2 minutes. Add seasoning and cook until sauce thickens. Add cashew nuts and stir well.

• Dish out and serve hot with rice.

RAINBOW VEGETABLE RICE

• PREPARATION TIME: 25 MIN • COOKING TIME: 20 MIN • SERVES 4

INGREDIENTS

Cooking oil	2 Tbsp
Ginger	2.5-cm knob, cut into strips
Garlic (optional)	3 cloves, cut into strips
Pumpkin	125 g, cut into small cubes
Carrot	180 g, cut into small cubes
Green peas	125 g
Red capsicum (bell pepper)	60 g, cored and cut into 1.5-cm cubes
Dried Chinese mushrooms	3, softened and cut into 1.5-cm cubes
Vegetarian oyster sauce	2 Tbsp
Sesame oil	1 Tbsp
Light soy sauce	2 Tbsp
Thai long-grain rice	500 g
Water	750 ml
Salt	1 tsp

METHOD

• Heat oil in a wok and fry ginger and garlic strips until light brown. Add all the vegetables and mushrooms and stir-fry for 2–3 minutes.

• Add oyster sauce, sesame oil and light soy sauce and stir well. Turn off heat.

• Place vegetable mixture and rice in a rice cooker. Add water and salt to taste. Cover and cook until rice is done. Serve hot.

CHEF'S NOTE

If you do not take garlic, omit it from this recipe.

From top: Kong Poh Mixed Vegetables (Spicy Mixed Vegetables), Rainbow Vegetable Rice

VEGETARIAN MINCED MEAT WITH BRINJALS

• PREPARATION TIME: 20 MIN • COOKING TIME: 20 MIN • SERVES 4

INGREDIENTS

Cooking oil	500 ml
Brinjals (aubergines/ eggplants)	6, quartered lengthwise and cut into 2.5-cm pieces
Preserved hot bean paste	1/2 Tbsp
Vegetarian minced meat	150 g, soaked and squeezed of excess water
Dried Chinese mushrooms	2 pieces, softened and minced
Onion	1, big, sliced
Spring onion (scallion)	1, cut into 2.5-cm lengths
Vegetable stock	125 ml (refer to page 82)
Cornflour	1 Tbsp, mixed with 1 Tbsp water

SEASONING

Sugar	2 Tbsp
Cooking oil	1 tsp
Light soy sauce	1 tsp
Thick soy sauce	1 tsp
Sesame oil	1/2 tsp

METHOD

• Heat oil in a pan and fry brinjals. Drain and set aside.

• Leaving 2 Tbsp oil in the pan, fry hot preserved bean paste until fragrant. Add vegetarian minced meat, minced mushrooms, onion slices and spring onions and mix well. Add vegetable stock and seasoning. Stir well and add fried brinjals.

• Lower heat and simmer until eggplants are soft. Add cornflour and stir well to thicken gravy. Dish out and serve hot.

MOCK HAR LOK (MOCK PRAWNS)

• PREPARATION TIME: 20 MIN • COOKING TIME: 15 MIN • SERVES 6

INGREDIENTS

Cooking oil	4 Tbsp
Garlic	3 cloves, chopped
Ginger	1.5-cm knob, sliced
Green chilli	2 Tbsp
Dark soy sauce	2 Tbsp
Tomato purée	1 Tbsp
Ground white pepper	1/2 Tbsp
Vegetarian oyster sauce	2 Tbsp
Sesame oil	1 Tbsp
Salt to taste	
Vegetarian mock prawns	500 g
Water	3 Tbsp
Egg	1, lightly beaten
Thin coconut milk	4 Tbsp (refer to page 82)
Cornflour	1 tsp, mixed with 1 Tbsp water
Spring onions (scallions)	4, cut into 2.5-cm lengths

METHOD

• Heat oil in a wok and add chopped garlic and ginger. Fry until aromatic. Add green chilli, dark soy sauce, tomato purée, pepper, oyster sauce, sesame oil and salt to taste. Fry until fragrant and stir well.

• Add mock prawns and mix well. Add water.

• Mix beaten egg with coconut milk and cornflour mixture. Pour into wok and cook for 2 minutes. Add spring onions and stir well. Serve hot.

CHEF'S NOTE

The egg in this recipe may be omitted for those who do not take eggs.

From top: Vegetarian Minced Meat with Brinjals, Mock Har Lok (Mock Prawns)

SIZZLING BEAN CURD

• PREPARATION TIME: 25 MIN • COOKING TIME: 30 MIN • SERVES 4

INGREDIENTS

Cooking oil	250 ml
Soft egg bean curd	3 rolls, each cut into 8 slices
Garlic	1 clove, chopped
Shallots	3, cut into cubes
Red chilli	1, cut into cubes
Dried Chinese mushrooms	2, softened and cut into cubes
Vegetarian soy minced meat	50 g, soaked and squeezed of excess water
Potato starch	1 Tbsp, mixed with 100 ml water
Egg	1, lightly beaten
Spring onion (scallion)	1, chopped

SEASONING

Sesame oil	1 1/2 Tbsp
Light soy sauce	2 Tbsp
Sugar	1 Tbsp
Hot bean sauce (tau pan)	1 Tbsp
Vegetarian oyster sauce	1 Tbsp
Water	4 Tbsp

METHOD

• Heat oil in a wok and fry bean curd slices until light brown. Drain and set aside.

• Leave 1 Tbsp oil in wok and fry garlic, shallots, red chillies and mushrooms. Stir well.

• Add minced meat and seasoning ingredients. Stir-fry for 2 minutes. Add potato starch mixture and stir to thicken gravy.

• Meanwhile, heat another wok and add 1 Tbsp oil. When oil is hot, add beaten egg and spread it around the wok evenly. Place fried bean curd mixture on top of egg and let it sizzle.

• Garnish with chopped spring onion and serve hot.

FRIED MOCK FISH WITH SPRING ONION AND GINGER

• PREPARATION TIME: 20 MIN • COOKING TIME: 15 MIN • SERVES 4

INGREDIENTS

Cooking oil	750 ml
Vegetarian mock fish	600 g, sliced thinly
Ginger	3-cm knob, sliced thinly
Red and green capsicums (bell peppers)	60 g each, cored and cut into 3-cm strips
Spring onions (scallion)	4, cut into 3-cm lengths

SEASONING

Vegetable stock	125 ml (refer to page 82)
Sugar	1 tsp
Potato flour	1 Tbsp
Ground white pepper	1 tsp

METHOD

• Heat oil in a wok and fry mock fish slices until brown. Drain and set aside.

• Leave 2 Tbsp oil in wok and fry ginger and capsicums for 1 minute. Add fried mock fish and seasoning ingredients. Mix well and bring to the boil. Cook for 2 minutes.

• Add spring onions and stir well. Dish out and serve hot with rice.

From top: Sizzling Bean Curd, Fried Mock Fish with Spring Onion and Ginger

STEAMED GLUTINOUS RICE IN LOTUS LEAF

• PREPARATION TIME: 30 MIN • COOKING TIME: 45 MIN • SERVES 6

INGREDIENTS

Lotus leaves	2, soaked in water for at least 4 hours to soften
Kitchen string	as needed
Glutinous rice	500 g, soaked for 6 hours and drained
Cooking oil	2 Tbsp
Vegetarian mock chicken	180 g
Dried Chinese mushrooms	8, softened and cut into 1.5-cm strips
Water chestnuts	100 g, cleaned and cut into 1-cm cubes
Green peas	125 g

SEASONING

Salt	1 tsp
Sugar	3 tsp
Dark soy sauce	2 Tbsp
Vegetarian oyster sauce	2 Tbsp
Sesame oil	2 tsp
Ground white pepper	1/2 tsp
Light soy sauce	1 Tbsp
Cooking oil	2 Tbsp

METHOD

• Steam glutinous rice for 20 minutes until half-cooked. Set aside to cool.

• Heat oil in a wok and stir-fry mock chicken until brown. Dish out, drain and set aside.

• In the same oil, fry mushrooms, water chestnuts and green peas.

• Combine fried mock chicken, mushrooms, water chestnuts and green peas in a large bowl. Add seasoning ingredients and mix well. Add steamed glutinous rice and mix again. Ensure ingredients are well distributed.

• Wipe softened lotus leaves dry. Place one leaf over the other.

• Spoon glutinous rice mixture onto centre of lotus leaves, then bring sides up over rice. Fold into a square parcel and secure with kitchen string.

• Steam for 30 minutes. Serve hot with chilli sauce.

FRIED DUMPLINGS

• PREPARATION TIME: 30 MIN • COOKING TIME: 25 MIN • SERVES 6

INGREDIENTS

Cooking oil	as needed

DOUGH

Plain flour	435 g
Glutinous flour	60 g
Cooking oil	4 Tbsp
Water	250 ml

FILLING

Vegetarian soy minced meat	200 g, soak in water and squeezed of excess water
Watercress	180 g, finely chopped
Chinese cabbage	180 g, finely chopped

SEASONING

Salt	1 tsp
Sugar	2 tsp
Ground white pepper	1/2 tsp

METHOD

• Combine plain flour, glutinous flour and oil in a bowl. Add water and mix until a dough comes together. Continue kneading until dough is smooth and pliable. Divide into 30 balls and set aside.

• Mix filling and seasoning ingredients together. Heat 1 Tbsp oil in a wok and fry filling until vegetables are tender and mixture is dry. Let cool, then divide into 15 portions.

• Roll dough balls out into flat round pieces. Spoon a portion of filling in the middle of a dough circle, then cover with another dough circle. Crimp edges to seal.

• Heat sufficient oil in a pan for shallow-frying, then fry dumplings in small batches until brown.

• Drain well and serve hot.

From top: Steamed Glutinous Rice in Lotus Leaf, Fried Dumplings

FRIED OYSTER MUSHROOMS IN SWEET AND SOUR SAUCE

• PREPARATION TIME: 30 MIN • COOKING TIME: 20 MIN • SERVES 6

INGREDIENTS

Oyster mushrooms	400 g
Salt	1½ tsp
Five-spice powder	½ tsp
Tapioca flour	200 g
Rice flour	200 g
Self-raising flour	200 g
Cooking oil for deep-frying	1 litre
Garlic	2 cloves, chopped
Tomato	1, cut into 1-cm cubes
Cucumber	½, cut into 1-cm cubes
Red and green capsicums (bell peppers)	60 g each, cored and cut into 1-cm cubes
Pineapple	¼, cut into 1-cm cubes
Tapioca flour	2 Tbsp, mixed with 2 Tbsp water

SAUCE

Tomato sauce	90 g
Chilli sauce	30 g
Plum sauce	30 g
Salt to taste	
Sugar	60 g
White vinegar	3 Tbsp
Water	250 ml

METHOD

• Marinate oyster mushrooms with salt and five-spice powder. Set aside for 15-20 minutes.

• Mix three types of flour in a big bowl. Dip mushrooms in flour mixture and coat thoroughly. Set aside.

• Heat oil in a wok and deep-fry mushrooms at high heat until golden brown. Drain and set aside.

• Leave 3 Tbsp oil in wok and stir-fry garlic, tomato, cucumber, capsicums and pineapple for 10 seconds. Add sauce ingredients and mix well. Bring to the boil, then stir in tapioca flour mixture to thicken gravy.

• When sauce is boiling, add fried mushrooms and mix. Dish out and serve hot.

From top: Fried Oyster Mushrooms in Sweet and Sour Sauce, Bean Curd Soup

BEAN CURD SOUP

• PREPARATION TIME: 25 MIN • COOKING TIME: 25 MIN • SERVES 6

INGREDIENTS

LIST A

Vegetable stock	1.25 litres (refer to page 82)
Sesame oil	2 Tbsp
Cream of mushroom soup	180 ml
Cornflour	50 g, mixed with 50 ml water
Fried chilli oil*	2 Tbsp
Egg	1, beaten

SEASONING

Salt	1 tsp
Sugar	1 tsp
Ground black pepper	2 Tbsp
Black vinegar	2 Tbsp
Ginger juice	2 Tbsp

LIST B

Soft bean curd	2 blocks, mashed finely
Straw mushrooms	50 g, cut into 0.5-cm lengths
Young bamboo shoots	30 g, cut into 0.5-cm lengths
Green chilli	1, cut into 0.5-cm cubes

METHOD

• In a pot, bring vegetable stock to the boil. Add cream of mushroom soup and seasoning. Stir well. Return to the boil and cook for another 2 minutes.

• Add ingredients under List B. Adjust to taste with salt. Stir well.

• Add cornflour mixture to thicken soup. Add beaten egg and stir well. Lastly add chilli oil and mix well. Serve hot.

*Fried Chilli Oil

INGREDIENTS

Cooking oil	125 ml
Dried chillies	50 g, seeds discarded; cut into small pieces

METHOD

• Heat oil in a wok and fry dried chillies until brown. Strain oil and discard chillies.

• Store chilli oil in an airtight jar.

KAH HEONG TAUFU POK
(DEEP-FRIED STUFFED BEAN CURD)
• PREPARATION TIME: 25 MIN • COOKING TIME: 25 MIN • SERVES 6

INGREDIENTS

Fried bean curd puffs	180 g
Potato	1, boiled and mashed finely
Sweet potato	1, boiled and mashed finely
Celery	30 g, cut into 0.5-cm cubes
Carrot	150 g, cut into 0.5-cm cubes
Turnip	120 g, cut into 0.5-cm cubes
Dried Chinese mushrooms	100 g, softened and cut into 0.5-cm cubes
Green peas	50 g
Cooking oil	750 ml

SEASONING

Salt	1/2 tsp
Water	4 Tbsp
Egg white	1, lightly beaten
Sugar	1 tsp

METHOD

• Make criss-cross cuts on top of bean curd puffs. Open puffs and remove white centres. Set aside.

• Combine mashed potato, sweet potato, celery, carrot, turnip and dried mushrooms. Add seasoning and mix well.

• Stuff mixture into bean curd puffs, then top with peas.

• Heat oil and deep-fry bean curd puffs until golden brown. Drain well.

• Serve hot or cold with special chilli sauce*.

*Special Chilli Sauce

INGREDIENTS

Ginger	1.5-cm knob
Garlic	4 cloves
Bird's eye chillies	10
Red chillies	6
Tomato sauce	30 g
Chilli sauce	30 g
Kalamansi juice	4 Tbsp
Salt	1 tsp or to taste
Sugar	3 Tbsp

METHOD

• Grind ginger, garlic, bird's eye chillies and red chillies together until fine. Combine with remaining ingredients and mix well. Adjust seasoning to taste.

STEWED MOCK MUTTON IN CLAYPOT
• PREPARATION TIME: 30 MIN • COOKING TIME: 40 MIN • SERVES 4

INGREDIENTS

Mock vegetarian mutton	500 g, soaked and drained
Cooking oil	180 ml
Vegetable stock	500 ml (refer to page 82)

SEASONING

Cinnamon	2 sticks
Star aniseed	3
Old ginger	2.5-cm knob, smashed
Salt	1 tsp
Vegetarian oyster sauce	2 Tbsp
Salt	1 tsp
Sugar	1 Tbsp
Sesame oil	2 Tbsp
Soda bicarbonate	1 tsp
Ginger juice	50 ml
Ground black pepper	1 tsp
Dark soy sauce	1 tsp
Cornflour	2 Tbsp

SAUCE

Worcester sauce	2 Tbsp
A1 steak sauce	2 Tbsp
Vegetarian oyster sauce	2 Tbsp
Sugar	2 Tbsp

METHOD

• Season mock mutton with seasoning ingredients and set aside for 20 minutes.

• Heat oil and deep-fry mock mutton until slightly brown.

• In a claypot, bring vegetable stock to the boil, then add seasoned mutton. Stew on slow heat until dry.

• Combine sauce ingredients and add to claypot. Leave to cool for 5 minutes. Serve hot with rice.

From top: Kah Heong Taufu Pok (Deep-fried Stuffed Bean Curd), Stewed Mock Mutton in Claypot

MIXED VEGETABLE KORMA

• PREPARATION TIME: 20 MIN • COOKING TIME: 20 MIN • SERVES 6

INGREDIENTS

Green banana	1, cut into cubes
Carrot	1, cut into cubes
Brinjals (aubergines/ eggplants)	2, cut into cubes
Potatoes	2, cut into cubes
Green peas	125 g
Long beans	200 g, cut into 2.5-cm lengths
Cauliflower	200 g, cut into florets
Cardamom	4 pods
Garlic	4 cloves
Ginger	2.5-cm knob
Poppy seeds	1 Tbsp
Grated coconut	150 g
Green chillies	4; 2 whole, 2 sliced
Tamarind pulp	100 g
Water	1 litre
Cooking oil	4 Tbsp
Onion	2, big, sliced
Turmeric powder	1 tsp
Chilli powder	1 Tbsp
Salt to taste	

METHOD

• Rinse vegetables and set aside.

• Grind cardamom, garlic, ginger, poppy seeds, grated coconut and 2 green chillies into a fine paste. Set aside.

• Mix tamarind pulp with 125 ml water and strain. Set aside.

• Heat oil in a pot and fry onions and sliced green chillies until onions turn brown.

• Add ground paste, turmeric powder and chilli powder and stir-fry to mix. Add vegetables, tamarind juice, remaining water and salt. Cover and cook for 10 minutes or until vegetables are tender.

• Serve hot with chappati or rice.

CAULIFLOWER BRIYANI

• PREPARATION TIME: 15 MIN • COOKING TIME: 25 MIN • SERVES 6

INGREDIENTS

Ghee (clarified butter)	60 g
Mustard seeds	1 tsp
Green chillies	6, sliced
Asafoetida	1/2 tsp
Curry leaves	2 sprigs
Big onions	2, sliced
Cashew nuts	125 g
Cauliflower	1 kg, cut into big florets
Water	1 litre
Yoghurt	180 ml
Turmeric powder	1 Tbsp
Salt to taste	
Coriander powder	1 Tbsp
Cumin powder	1 Tbsp
Amti masala powder	2 Tbsp (refer to page 83)
Basmati rice	750 g
Grated coconut	50 g
Coriander (cilantro) leaves	2 sprigs, chopped
Lemon	1, sliced

METHOD

• Heat ghee in a rice cooker. Add mustard seeds and when it splutters, add green chillies, asafoetida, curry leaves, onions, cashew nuts and cauliflower. Fry until onions are soft.

• Add water, yoghurt, turmeric powder and salt to taste. Stir well.

• Add coriander, cumin and amti masala powders. Stir well, then add rice. Boil until water is evaporated and rice is fluffy and done.

• Garnish with fresh grated coconut, chopped coriander leaves and lemon slices. Serve hot.

From top: Mixed Vegetable Korma, Cauliflower Briyani

DHAL ROLLS IN BUTTERMILK GRAVY

• PREPARATION TIME: 45 MIN • COOKING TIME: 15 MIN • SERVES 6

INGREDIENTS

DHAL ROLLS

Gram dhal	250 g
Bengal gram dhal	65 g
Grated coconut	100 g
Turmeric powder	1 tsp
Garam masala powder	2 tsp (refer to page 83)
Salt to taste	
Green chillies	2, chopped finely
Onions	2, big, chopped finely
Curry leaves	8 sprigs, chopped finely
Coriander (cilantro) leaves	100 g, chopped finely
Breadcrumbs	2 Tbsp

BUTTERMILK GRAVY

Yoghurt	500 ml
Gram flour	125 g, sieved
Water	125 ml
Onion	1, big, cut into cubes
Green chillies	2, chopped
Grated coconut	1 Tbsp
Cumin seeds	1 tsp
Turmeric powder	1 tsp
Salt to taste	
Sugar	1 Tbsp
Cooking oil	2 Tbsp
Mustard seeds	1 tsp
Red chillies	2, sliced in half lengthwise
Curry leaves	2 sprigs
Coriander (cilantro) leaves	2 sprigs

METHOD

• To make dhal rolls, soak both types of dhal in water for 2 hours. Drain and grind to a coarse paste. Add remaining ingredients and mix well. Add salt to taste.

• Shape paste into long rolls and steam for 30 minutes until done. Remove and slice thickly. Set aside.

• To make buttermilk *kadhi*, mix yoghurt and gram flour with 125 ml water until a gravy-like consistency is reached. Add onions, green chillies, coconut and cumin seeds and churn the mixture well. Add turmeric powder, salt, sugar and stir well.

• In a pot, heat oil and add mustard seeds, red chillies, curry leaves. Fry till aromatic. Add yoghurt mixture and coriander leaves. Boil for 5 minutes, adding more water if required to maintain gravy-like consistency. Add dhal slices and simmer for another 2 minutes.

• Dish out and serve hot.

PLANTAIN PERETTAL (STIR-FRIED GREEN BANANA)

• PREPARATION TIME: 15 MIN • COOKING TIME: 20 MIN • SERVES 4

INGREDIENTS

Green bananas	6
Ghee (clarified butter)	75 g
Big onions	2, sliced
Garlic	3 cloves, chopped
Green chillies	3, halved
Water	125 ml
Ground cumin	1 tsp
Turmeric powder	1 tsp
Chilli powder	2 Tbsp
Grated coconut	50 g
Salt to taste	
Curry leaves	2 sprigs

METHOD

• Peel bananas and cut into 2.5-cm cubes. Soak in cold salted water for 5 minutes. Drain and set aside.

• Heat ghee in a frying pan and fry onions, garlic and green chillies until brown. Add bananas and water and stir well. Cook over a slow fire until bananas are tender.

• Add cumin, turmeric and chilli powders, followed by grated coconut. Season with salt to taste. Cook until gravy is dry.

• Dish out and garnish with curry leaves. Serve hot with rice or chilled.

From top: Plantain Perettal (Stir-fried Green Bananas), Dhal Rolls in Buttermilk Gravy

MINT RICE

- PREPARATION TIME: 15 MIN • COOKING TIME: 25 MIN • SERVES 6

INGREDIENTS

Mint leaves	200 g
Shallots	150 g, peeled
Ghee (clarified butter)	100 g
Cashew nuts	125 g
Basmati rice	840 g
Mature ginger	5-cm knob, extract juice
Thin coconut milk	1.5 litres (refer to page 82)
Salt to taste	
Fried onions	100 g

METHOD

- Grind mint leaves and shallots together until fine. Set aside.

- Heat ghee in a rice cooker and fry cashew nuts until light brown. Dish out and set aside.

- Place rice, ground mint leaves and shallots and ginger juice into the rice cooker. Mix well. Add thin coconut milk and salt to taste. Cover and cook until rice is done.

- Dish out, garnish with fried onions. Serve with curries.

FRIED STUFFED SNAKE GOURD

- PREPARATION TIME: 20 MIN • COOKING TIME: 20 MIN • SERVES 4

INGREDIENTS

Minced vegetarian mutton	125 g
Snake gourd	1, cut into 10-cm pieces, seeds removed
Cooking oil	3 Tbsp
Garlic	3 cloves, chopped
Curry leaves	1 sprig, cut finely
Onion	1, cut into small cubes
French beans	200 g, cut into small cubes
Red chilli	1, cut into small cubes
Carrot	1, cut into small cubes
Green peas	150 g
Garam masala	1 tsp
Turmeric powder	1 tsp
Salt to taste	
Water	125 ml
Gram dhal	100 g, boiled
Gram dhal powder	250 g
Cooking oil for deep-frying	500 ml

METHOD

- Soak minced vegetarian mutton for 30 minutes and squeeze dry. Wash 2–3 times to remove any smells. Parboil snake gourd pieces in salted water for 5 minutes. Drain and set aside.

- Heat 3 Tbsp oil in a frying pan. Fry garlic, curry leaves and onion until soft. Add French beans, red chilli, carrot and green peas and stir well. Add minced vegetarian mutton, garam masala, turmeric powder, salt and water and stir. Cook until dry.

- Add cooked gram dhal and 2 Tbsp gram dhal powder to thicken mixture. Fill snake gourd with mixture.

- Add some water and 1/2 tsp salt to remaining gram dhal powder to make a thick paste.

- Heat oil for deep-frying in a frying pan.

- Dip stuffed snake gourd in gram dhal paste, then lower into hot oil and fry in batches until brown. Drain well.

- Cut into 5-cm lengths and serve.

From top: Mint Rice, Fried Stuffed Snake Gourd

MUGALAI VEGETABLE PILAU
• PREPARATION TIME: 20 MIN • COOKING TIME: 25 MIN • SERVES 6

INGREDIENTS

Basmati rice	750 g
French beans	200 g, cut into 2.5-cm lengths
Carrot	1, quartered lengthways and cut into 2.5-cm sticks
Grated coconut	3 Tbsp
Poppy seeds (optional)	1¹/₂ Tbsp
Green chillies	10
Cashew nuts	120 g, roasted
Garlic	8 cloves
Coriander seeds	4 Tbsp
Ginger	3.5-cm knob
Ghee (clarified butter)	100 g
Cloves	5
Cardamom	4 pods
Cinnamon	5-cm stick
Raisins	60 g
Mixed fresh fruits	375 g, diced
Butter	75 g, melted

METHOD

• Cook rice in a rice cooker; then cool and spread the grains.

• Blanch beans and carrot. Set aside.

• Grind grated coconut, poppy seeds, green chillies, half portion of cashew nuts, garlic, coriander seeds and ginger to make masala. Set aside.

• Heat ghee in a wok. Add cloves, cardamom, cinnamon, raisins and remaining cashew nuts. Fry until aromatic. Add ground masala and continue to fry until oil rises to the top.

• Add blanched vegetables and stir-fry. Add cooked rice and mix well.

• Remove from heat and add diced fruits and melted butter. Mix well and serve hot.

MUSALAM PHOOL GOBI (FRIED MASALA CAULIFLOWER)
• PREPARATION TIME: 15 MIN • COOKING TIME: 20 MIN • SERVES 6

INGREDIENTS

Cauliflower	800 g, cut into big florets
Garlic	4 cloves
Ginger	2.5-cm knob
Poppy seeds (optional)	1¹/₂ Tbsp
Grated coconut	2 Tbsp
Cashew nuts	80 g
Ghee (clarified butter)	125 g
Big onions	4, sliced
Cinnamon	2.5-cm length
Cardamom	3 pods
Curry leaves	1 sprig
Tomatoes	3, cut into big cubes
Chilli powder	1¹/₂ Tbsp
Yoghurt	125 ml

METHOD

• Half steam the cauliflower florets. Set aside.

• Grind garlic, ginger, poppy seeds, grated coconut and cashew nuts together until fine. Set aside.

• Heat ghee in a wok and fry onions until brown. Drain and set aside.

• In the same wok, fry cinnamon, cardamoms, curry leaves and ground ingredients until aromatic. Add tomatoes, chilli powder and yoghurt and cook for another 5 minutes.

• When gravy is thick, add steamed cauliflower and cook over slow fire for another 5 minutes. Add fried onions and mix well.

• Serve hot with rice or chappati.

From top: Musalam Phool Gobi (Fried Masala Cauliflower), Mugalai Vegetable Pilau

PAKORA CURD CURRY

• PREPARATION TIME: 20 MIN • COOKING TIME: 25 MIN • SERVES 6

INGREDIENTS

Cooking oil for deep-frying 1 litre

FRIED PAKORAS

Bengal gram dhal	65 g
Turmeric powder	1/2 tsp
Big onions	1, cut into cubes
Salt to taste	
Chilli powder	1/2 tsp
A pinch of baking soda	
Water	375 ml

CURD CURRY

Yoghurt	375 ml
Bengal gram dhal	1 1/2 Tbsp
Water	1 litre
Ghee (clarified butter)	75 g
Fenugreek seeds	1/2 tsp
Cumin seeds	1/2 tsp
Mustard seeds	1/2 tsp
Asafoetida	1/4 tsp
Green chillies	4, each halved
Turmeric powder	1/2 tsp
Ginger	2.5-cm knob, cubed
Curry leaves	1 sprig
Chilli powder	1 1/2 tsp
Salt to taste	

METHOD

• Combine ingredients for fried pakora to obtain a thick batter.

• Heat oil for deep-frying. Drop spoonfuls of batter into hot oil and fry until batter floats and is brown. Drain and set aside.

• To make curd curry, beat yoghurt, dhal and water together.

• Heat ghee and add fenugreek, cumin and mustard seeds along with asafoetida and green chillies. Fry until aromatic.

• Add turmeric powder, ginger, curry leaves, chilli powder and salt to taste. Add yoghurt mixture and bring to the boil.

• Add fried pakoras and cook over slow heat until gravy is thick. Serve hot.

SPECIAL PARUPU SAMBAR (SPECIAL DHAL CURRY)

• PREPARATION TIME: 15 MIN • COOKING TIME: 30 MIN • SERVES 6

INGREDIENTS

Water	1 litre
Gram dhal	250 g
Turmeric powder	1 tsp
Garlic	3 cloves, quartered
Salt to taste	
Cooking oil	3 Tbsp
Mustard seeds	1 tsp
Asafoetida	1/4 tsp
Curry leaves	1 sprig
Sambar powder	3 Tbsp (refer to page 83)
Tamarind pulp	80 g, soaked in 125 ml water and strained
Carrot	1, cut into rounds
Potatoes	2, quartered
Round brinjals (aubergines/eggplants)	2, cut into wedges
Green chillies	2, split lengthwise
Red chillies	2, split lengthwise
Tomatoes	2, cut into wedges

METHOD

• Boil gram dhal in water. Add turmeric powder, garlic and salt. Cook until dhal is soft.

• Heat oil in a pot and add mustard seeds. When it crackles, add asafoetida and curry leaves. Stir well.

• Add sambar powder and fry until aromatic. Add tamarind juice, cooked dhal, carrot, potatoes and brinjals. Add water if needed. Cook until vegetables are done.

• Add chillies and tomatoes and continue to boil for another 5 minutes. Serve hot with rice.

CHEF'S NOTE

Other vegetables such as radish, marrow and drumsticks can also be added to this dish. Add them together with the carrots and brinjals.

From top: Pakora Curd Curry, Special Parupu Sambar (Special Dhal Curry)

PALAK PANEER
(SPINACH WITH COTTAGE CHEESE)
• PREPARATION TIME: 20 MIN • COOKING TIME: 25 MIN • SERVES 4

INGREDIENTS

PANEER

Fresh milk	1 litre
Lime juice	extracted from 2 limes

PALAK

Cooking oil	3 Tbsp
Onions	2, big, sliced
Chilli powder	1 Tbsp
Green chillies	3, sliced
Salt to taste	
Spinach	1 kg, cut into 1-cm lengths
Water	180 ml
Garlic	3 cloves, sliced thinly
Ginger	2.5-cm knob, sliced thinly

METHOD

• To prepare paneer, bring milk to the boil and add lime juice. Allow mixture to curdle. Pour into a bowl lined with muslin cloth and use the muslin cloth to squeeze the curd dry.

• Place something heavy over muslin-covered paneer and set aside for 1 hour. Cut paneer into 1-cm cubes and set aside.

• To prepare *palak*, heat oil in a pot. Fry onions until slightly brown. Add chilli powder, green chillies and salt. Stir well. Add spinach, water, ginger and garlic. Cover and cook until spinach is soft.

• Mash cooked spinach and stir well. Add cubed paneer. Bring mixture to the boil and cook for 2 minutes.

• Serve hot with chappati or naan.

KERALA VEGETABLE AVIYAL
(KERALA MIXED VEGETABLE CURRY)
• PREPARATION TIME: 20 MIN • COOKING TIME: 20 MIN • SERVES 6

INGREDIENTS

Green banana	1, diced
Potatoes	2, diced
French beans	15, diced
Brinjal (aubergine/ eggplant)	1, large, diced
Carrot	1, diced
Cauliflower	200 g, cut into florets
Drumsticks	3, cut into 2.5-cm pieces
Turmeric powder	$1/2$ tsp
Chilli powder	1 Tbsp
Salt to taste	
Water	250 ml
Yoghurt	125 ml
Green chillies	4
Fresh grated coconut	100 g
Big onions	2; 1 whole, 1 sliced
Ghee (clarified butter)	115 g
Mustard seeds	1 tsp
Dried chillies	3, halved
Curry leaves	1 sprig

METHOD

• Place cut vegetables, turmeric powder, chilli powder and salt in a pot. Add water and cook until water is evaporated and vegetables are half-cooked. Add yoghurt and mix well. Set aside.

• Grind green chillies, grated coconut and whole onion into a fine paste. Set aside.

• Heat ghee in a wok. Add mustard seeds, dried chillies, curry leaves, sliced onion. Stir-fry until onion slices turn brown. Add ground paste and fry until aromatic.

• Add vegetables and stir well. Continue to cook for 5 minutes. Serve hot with rice.

From top: Kerala Vegetable Aviyal (Kerala Mixed Vegetable Curry), Palak Paneer (Spinach with Cottage Cheese)

MOORU KOLUMBU
(BUTTERMILK CURRY)
• PREPARATION TIME: 20 MIN • COOKING TIME: 15 MIN • SERVES 6

INGREDIENTS

Ginger	1-cm knob
Green chillies	2
Red chillies	2
Cumin seeds	1 Tbsp
Gram dhal flour	2 Tbsp
Turmeric powder	1/2 tsp
Yoghurt	750 ml
Water	250 ml
Yellow pumpkin	250 g, cut into 2.5-cm cubes
French beans	250 g, cut into 2.5-cm cubes
Raw banana	1, cut into 2.5-cm cubes
Drumsticks (optional)	2, cut into 5-cm lengths
Curry leaves	2 sprigs
Cooking oil	2 Tbsp
Mustard seeds	1 tsp
Dried chillies	3, cut into 2.5-cm lengths

METHOD

• Grind ginger, green and red chillies and cumin seeds together into a fine paste. Set aside.

• In a pot, mix the gram dhal, turmeric powder, yoghurt and water together. Bring the mixture to boil. Add the vegetables, grounded paste, curry leaves and simmer for 8 minutes.

• In a frying pan, add oil and fry the mustard seeds and dried chillies until aromatic. Add to the yoghurt mixture, and stir well.

• Dish out and serve hot with rice.

BRINJAL CHUTNEY
• PREPARATION TIME: 15 MIN • COOKING TIME: 15 MIN • SERVES 6

INGREDIENTS

Long brinjals (aubergines /eggplants)	1 kg
Turmeric powder	1/2 tsp
Salt to taste	
Cooking oil	250 ml
Big onions	2-3, sliced
Cinnamon	5-cm length
Cardamom	3 pods
Pandan (screwpine) leaves	2
Cloves	3
Meat curry powder	1 1/2 Tbsp
Tamarind juice	125 ml, obtained from 85 g tamarind pulp
Sugar	45 g or to taste
Thick coconut milk	1/2 portion (refer to page 82)
Coriander (cilantro) leaves	1 sprig, chopped

METHOD

• Cut brinjals into 10-cm lengths and marinate with turmeric powder and salt. In a deep frying pan, heat oil and fry brinjals until brown. Set aside.

• Leave 3 Tbsp oil in pan and fry sliced onions, cinnamon, cardamom, pandan leaves, cloves and curry powder until aromatic.

• Add tamarind juice, sugar, salt and coconut milk. Cook for 5 minutes. Add fried brinjals and stir well. Cook for another 3 minutes.

• Dish out and garnish with chopped coriander leaves. Serve with rice or chappati.

CHEF'S NOTE
Long brinjals can be substituted with the round variety. Alternatively, use breadfruit.

From top: Mooru Kolumbu (Buttermilk Curry), Brinjal Chutney

BRINJAL AND PINEAPPLE CURRY
• PREPARATION TIME: 25 MIN • COOKING TIME: 20 MIN • SERVES 4

INGREDIENTS

Pineapple	1
Brinjals (aubergines/ eggplants)	2
Water	250 ml
Grated coconut	125 g
Fermented soy bean paste	1 Tbsp
Coriander (cilantro) roots	3
Galangal	6 slices
Lemongrass (serai)	5 stalks
Shallots	8
Garlic	8 cloves
Kaffir lime rind	1/2 tsp, grated
Dried chillies	18, softened in hot water
Boiled coconut cream	1 portion (refer to page 82)
Light soy sauce	3 Tbsp
Palm sugar (gula melaka)	2 Tbsp

METHOD

• Clean, core and slice pineapple into rings.

• Split brinjals lengthwise and cut into 5-cm lengths.

• Add water to grated coconut and extract milk. Set aside.

• Grind fermented soy bean paste, coriander roots, galangal, lemongrass, shallots, garlic, grated kaffir lime rind and dried chillies finely. Heat coconut cream in a pot and fry ground ingredients, light soy sauce and palm sugar until aromatic and oil rises to the top.

• Add brinjals and coconut milk. Allow to boil until brinjals are half-cooked. Add pineapple rings and simmer for 2 minutes. Serve hot.

SAVOURY VEGETABLE FRITTERS
• PREPARATION TIME: 20 MIN • COOKING TIME: 20 MIN • SERVES 4

INGREDIENTS

Rice flour	1 Tbsp
Plain flour	250 g
Cornflour	2 Tbsp
Baking powder	1/2 tsp
Ground pepper	1/2 tsp
Water	125 ml
Sesame oil	1/2 tsp
Cooking oil	1 Tbsp
Salt to taste	
Dried Chinese mushrooms	50 g, softened in hot water and cut into 1-cm cubes
Carrots	80 g, cut into 1-cm cubes
Bean sprouts	50 g
Chinese chives	50 g, chopped
Green peas	50 g
Basil leaves	25 g, chopped
Cooking oil for deep-frying	1 litre

METHOD

• Combine rice flour, plain flour, cornflour, baking powder and ground pepper in a bowl. Add water and mix into a smooth paste.

• Add sesame oil, 1 Tbsp oil and salt. Mix well. Add mushrooms and vegetables and mix into batter.

• Heat oil for deep-frying. Drop tablespoonfuls of batter into hot oil and deep-fry until fritters float and are golden brown. Cook in small batches.

• Drain well. Serve with garlic chilli sauce*.

*GARLIC CHILLI SAUCE

INGREDIENTS

Red chillies	8
Garlic	4 cloves
Salt	1/2 tsp
White vinegar	3 Tbsp
Sugar	125 g

METHOD

• Combine ingredients and blend together until fine. Store in an airtight container in the fridge.

From top: Brinjal and Pineapple Curry, Savoury Vegetable Fritters

SPICY PEANUT BUTTER SALAD

· PREPARATION TIME: 25 MIN · SERVES 4

INGREDIENTS

SAUCE

Garlic	2 cloves, chopped finely
Lime juice	extracted from 4 limes
Light soy sauce	3 Tbsp
Salt to taste	
Ground dried chillies	1 Tbsp
Sugar	2 Tbsp
Peanut butter	4 Tbsp

SALAD

Red and green capsicums (bell peppers)	1 each, small, cored and cut into strips
Celery	100 g, cut into 2.5-cm lengths
Button mushrooms	200 g, halved
Carrot	180 g, cut into 2.5-cm lengths
Water chestnuts	200 g, cut into 2.5-cm cubes

METHOD

· In a bowl, mix together ingredients for sauce. Add cut vegetables and toss well. Adjust seasoning to taste.

· Serve cold.

LADNA RICE

· PREPARATION TIME: 20 MIN · COOKING TIME: 15 MIN · SERVES 2

INGREDIENTS

Cooked rice	500 g
Cooking oil	3 Tbsp
Garlic	2 cloves, chopped
Oyster mushrooms	200 g, cut into broad strips
Wood ear fungus	1 piece, soaked in water
Button mushrooms	200 g, halved
Soft bean curd	1 block, cut into small cubes and fried
Water chestnuts	200 g, cut into 1-cm cubes
Canned green peas	100 g
Kaffir lime leaves	2, torn into pieces
Tomato	1, cut into 2.5-cm cubes
Mock vegetarian chicken	100 g
Vegetable stock	500 ml (refer to page 82)
Sugar	1 Tbsp
Light soy sauce	2 Tbsp
Ground black pepper	1 tsp
Cornflour	2 Tbsp, mix with 2 Tbsp water
Spring onion (scallion)	1, cut into 2.5-cm lengths

METHOD

· Divide cooked rice into two portions and place on two plates. Set aside.

· Heat oil in a wok and fry garlic until golden brown. Add oyster mushrooms, wood ear fungus, button mushrooms, bean curd, chestnuts, peas, lime leaves, tomato and mock chicken. Stir-fry over high heat for 2 minutes.

· Add stock and season with sugar, soy sauce and black pepper. Stir well and thicken with cornflour mixture.

· Ladle mixture equally over plates of rice and garnish with chopped spring onion. Serve with chopped bird's eye chillies or pickled chillies, if desired.

CHEF'S NOTE

Garlic can be substituted with ginger in this recipe.

CORN AND VEGETABLE PATTIES

• PREPARATION TIME: 20 MIN • COOKING TIME: 20 MIN • SERVES 4

INGREDIENTS

Eggs	2, large, lightly beaten
Corn kernels	750 g
Cornflour	1 Tbsp
Plain flour	2 Tbsp
Rice flour	2 Tbsp
Long beans	150 g, thinly sliced
Hot chilli paste	2 Tbsp (refer to page 82)
Light soy sauce	2 Tbsp
Salt to taste	
Coriander (cilantro) leaves	1 sprig, cut into small pieces
Cooking oil for frying	750 ml

METHOD

• In a bowl, mix all the ingredients, except oil, together. Adjust with salt to taste.

• Take a scoop of the mixture, about the size of a golf ball, and shape it into a patty. Repeat with remaining mixture.

• Heat oil in a wok and fry patties until golden brown. Drain and serve hot.

PUMPKIN AND MOCK CHICKEN CURRY

• PREPARATION TIME: 20 MIN • COOKING TIME: 15 MIN • SERVES 4

INGREDIENTS

Dried chillies	10, softened in hot water
Shallots	6
Garlic	10 cloves
Galangal	1-cm knob
Lemongrass (serai)	2 stalks
Kaffir lime rind	1/2 tsp
Coriander (cilantro) roots	3
White peppercorns	10
Cooking oil	250 ml
Vegetarian mock chicken	300 g, cleaned
Grated coconut	30 g, mixed with 250 ml water and squeezed to extract milk
Palm sugar (gula melaka)	2 Tbsp
Kaffir lime leaves	2
Light soy sauce	3 Tbsp
Pumpkin	600 g, cut into 2.5-cm cubes
Coriander (cilantro) leaves	1 sprig, chopped

METHOD

• Grind dried chillies, shallots, garlic, galangal, lemongrass, kaffir lime rind, coriander roots and white peppercorns together into a fine paste. Set aside.

• Heat oil in a pan and fry mock chicken pieces until golden brown. Drain and set aside.

• Leave 2 Tbsp oil in pan and fry ground paste until fragrant. Add coconut milk and continue frying until oil rises to the top.

• Add palm sugar, kaffir lime leaves and soy sauce. Stir to mix well. Add pumpkin and stir. Cover and cook until pumpkin is almost done.

• Add fried mock chicken and continue to cook for another 2 minutes.

• Garnish with coriander leaves and serve hot.

From top: Corn and Vegetable Patties, Pumpkin and Mock Chicken Curry

CRISP-FRIED OKRAS IN BATTER

• PREPARATION TIME: 10 MIN • COOKING TIME: 20 MIN • SERVES 4

INGREDIENTS

Cornflour	70 g
Egg yolk	1
Thick coconut milk	180 ml (*refer to page 82*)
Salt	1/2 tsp
Turmeric powder	1/2 tsp
Cooking oil	625 ml
Okras (lady's fingers)	500 g, cut into 1-cm lengths
Lettuce	5-6 leaves

METHOD

• Stir together cornflour, egg yolk, coconut milk, salt and turmeric powder to obtain a batter.

• Heat oil in a wok. Dip okra pieces in batter and fry until golden brown. Drain.

• Serve hot on a plate of lettuce leaves.

CHEF'S NOTE

Besides okras, this recipe can also be prepared with pumpkin, sweet potatoes, oyster mushrooms, long beans or any leafy vegetable.

SAUTÉED YOUNG JACKFRUIT

• PREPARATION TIME: 30 MIN • COOKING TIME: 20 MIN • SERVES 4

INGREDIENTS

Young jackfruit	375 g
Water	1 litre
Cooking oil	2 Tbsp
Garlic	3 cloves, chopped
Lemongrass (*serai*)	2 stalks, sliced thinly
Bird's eye chillies	3, sliced
Vegetarian chilli paste	3 Tbsp (*refer to page 82*)
Evaporated milk	2 Tbsp
Chinese celery	2 stalks, cut into 2.5-cm lengths
Lettuce	50 g, shredded
Tomato	1

SEASONING

Sugar	1 tsp
Light soy sauce	2 Tbsp
Cream of mushroom soup	125 ml

METHOD

• Clean jackfruit and cut into chunky pieces.

• Bring water to the boil. Add jackfruit and boil for 15 minutes to cook. Drain and set aside.

• Heat oil in a wok. Add garlic, lemongrass and bird's eye chillies and mix well. Add chilli paste and continue to fry until aromatic.

• Add jackfruit pieces and stir well for a few minutes.

• Add evaporated milk, Chinese celery, lettuce, tomato and seasoning ingredients. Stir well and cook for 2 minutes. Dish out and serve hot.

From Left: Crisp Fried Okras in Batter, Sautéed Young Jackfruit

SAVOURY MARROW AND POTATO SOUP

• PREPARATION TIME: 25 MIN • COOKING TIME: 20 MIN • SERVES 4

INGREDIENTS

Vegetable stock	1.5 litres (*refer to page 82*)
Lesser ginger (*krachai*)	3 roots
Hot chilli paste	1 Tbsp (*refer to page 82*)
Fried chilli oil	1 Tbsp (*refer to page 34*)
Palm sugar (*gula melaka*)	1 Tbsp
Light soy sauce	3 Tbsp
Salt to taste	
Marrow	1, about 300 g, cut into 5-cm cubes
Potato	1, cleaned and cut into 2.5-cm cubes
Carrot	1, cleaned and cut into floral shapes
Corn kernels	125 g, rinsed and drained
Sweet basil leaves	2 sprigs, chopped

METHOD

• Pour vegetable stock into a stockpot and add lesser ginger, chilli paste, fried chilli oil, palm sugar, light soy sauce and salt. Bring to the boil.

• Add marrow, potatoes and carrots and boil until vegetables are tender.

• Add corn kernels and basil leaves. Let soup come to a simmer before serving.

THAI-STYLE FRIED MOCK FISH WITH SAUCE

• PREPARATION TIME: 25 MIN • COOKING TIME: 20 MIN • SERVES 4

INGREDIENTS

Vegetarian mock fish fillet	500 g, cut into 1.5-cm slices
Cooking oil	500 ml

SEASONING

Salt	1/2 tsp
Sugar	1 tsp
Egg	1
Plain flour	2 Tbsp
Cornflour	1 Tbsp

SAUCE

Lime juice	435 ml
Bird's eye chillies	30 g, chopped into small pieces
Lemongrass (*serai*)	4 stalks, sliced into small pieces
Torch ginger flower	1 stalk, sliced into small pieces
Coriander (cilantro) leaves	2 sprigs, cut into 1-cm lengths
Plum sauce	300 ml
Vegetarian oyster sauce	300 ml
Sugar	250 g
Salt	1 tsp

METHOD

• Marinate mock fish with seasoning ingredients for about 1 hour.

• Meanwhile make sauce. Combine all ingredients in a pot and bring to the boil. Set aside.

• Heat oil in a wok and fry seasoned mock fish until brown. Drain and set aside.

• Arrange fried mock fish on a plate and pour cooked sauce over. Garnish with shredded lemongrass and chilli. Serve hot.

From top: Savoury Marrow and Potato Soup, Thai-Style Fried Mock Fish with Sauce

MIXED VEGETABLE OMELETTE

• PREPARATION TIME: 20 MIN • COOKING TIME: 15 MIN • SERVES 3

INGREDIENTS

Eggs	3
Cooking oil	4 Tbsp
Garlic	2 cloves, chopped finely
Straw mushrooms	100 g
Firm bean curd	1, cut into 0.5-cm cubes
French beans	50 g, cut into 0.5-cm lengths
Water chestnuts	100 g, cut into 0.5-cm cubes
Green peas	50 g
Small carrot	1, cut into 0.5-cm cubes
Sweet basil leaves	20 g, chopped
Bird's eye chillies	2, cut into small pieces
Light soy sauce	2 Tbsp
Sugar	2 tsp
Potato flour	2 Tbsp, mixed with 1 Tbsp water
Salt to taste	

METHOD

• Break eggs into a bowl. Whisk lightly and set aside.

• Heat half the oil in a wok and fry garlic until fragrant. Add mushrooms, bean curd and vegetables and stir-fry over high heat for 2 minutes. Season with light soy sauce and sugar. Mix well and set aside to cool.

• To beaten eggs, add potato flour mixture and salt. Mix well.

• Heat remaining oil in a non-stick pan. Ladle a third of egg mixture into pan and swirl pan to spread mixture into a sheet. Top with a third of the vegetable mixture. When egg is set, fold it in half. Carefully dish out.

• Repeat process with remaining egg and vegetables. Serve hot.

CHEF'S NOTE

Change up the vegetables in the omelette with your favourite ingredients. The basil leaves can be fried separately until crisp and added to the omelette before folding.

VEGETABLE BEAN CURD SOUP

• PREPARATION TIME: 20 MIN • COOKING TIME: 15 MIN • SERVES 4

INGREDIENTS

Vegetable stock	750 ml (refer to page 82)
Young ginger	3 slices
Salted radish	100 g, diced
Carrot	1, sliced
Soft bean curd	2 blocks, cut into 2.5-cm cubes
Glass noodles	50 g, soaked in water
Green peas	50 g
Wood ear fungus	1 piece, softened in hot water
Straw mushrooms	100 g
Button mushrooms	200 g
Ground white pepper	1 tsp
Salt to taste	
Light soy sauce	2 Tbsp
Garlic	2 cloves, chopped and fried

METHOD

• Pour vegetable stock into a pot and bring to the boil. Add ginger, salted radish, carrot, bean curd, noodles, peas, wood ear fungus, straw mushrooms and button mushrooms. Let stock return to the boil.

• Season with pepper, salt and soy sauce. Stir to mix well.

• Ladle into serving bowls and garnish with fried garlic.

CHEF'S NOTE

Leafy vegetables can be added to the soup if desired.

From top: Mixed Vegetable Omelette, Vegetable Bean Curd Soup

STEAMED SOFT BEAN CURD WITH THAI SAUCE

• PREPARATION TIME: 20 MIN • COOKING TIME: 20 MIN • SERVES 2

INGREDIENTS

Soft bean curd	2 blocks
Ginger	1-cm knob
Coriander (cilantro) roots	4
Garlic	5 cloves
White peppercorns	10
Cooking oil	4 Tbsp
Fermented soy bean paste	3 Tbsp, minced
Dried soy minced meat	50 g, soaked in hot water and drained
Kaffir lime leaf	1, cut very finely
Sugar	2 Tbsp
Light soy sauce	2 Tbsp

METHOD

• Make criss-cross slits across each bean curd piece, taking care not to break it. Place on a banana leaf-lined plate. Set aside.

• Grind ginger, coriander roots, garlic and peppercorns until fine.

• Heat oil in a wok and add fermented soy bean paste, ground ingredients and minced meat. Fry until aromatic.

• Add kaffir lime leaf, sugar, light soy sauce and cook until sauce is slightly thick.

• Pour sauce on top of bean curd pieces and place plate in a steamer. Cover and steam for 10 minutes. Serve hot.

DUMPLINGS AND VEGETABLES IN COCONUT MILK SOUP

• PREPARATION TIME: 20 MIN • COOKING TIME: 20 MIN • SERVES 5

INGREDIENTS

DUMPLINGS

Vegetarian minced meat	100 g, softened in hot water for 30 minutes
Cornflour	2 Tbsp
Small carrot	1, cut into small cubes
Coriander (cilantro) leaves	1 sprig, cut into small pieces
Bird's eye chillies	2, cut into small pieces
Soft bean curd	1 block, mashed finely
Light soy sauce	2 Tbsp
Sesame oil	1 tsp
Salt to taste	
Plain flour	1 Tbsp
Wonton skins	25 pieces

SOUP

Thin coconut milk	1 portion (refer to page 82)
Spinach	200 g, cut into 5-cm lengths
Carrot	1, sliced into rounds
Chinese cabbage	200 g, cut into 5-cm pieces
Bean curd	2 blocks, cut into 5-cm long pieces
Sugar	2 Tbsp
Salt to taste	
Bird's eye chillies	6, bruised slightly
Kaffir lime leaves	6
Lime juice	extracted from 2 limes

METHOD

• Mix all dumpling ingredients, except wonton skins, together to form a smooth paste. Place a small spoonful of paste onto a wonton skin and bring the edges together. Seal with a little water and flour mixture. Continue until all the ingredients are used up. Set aside.

• To make soup, place coconut milk in a pot and bring to the boil. Add dumplings and cook for 3–4 minutes. Remove dumplings and set aside.

• Add spinach, carrot, Chinese cabbage, bean curd, sugar, salt, bird's eye chillies and kaffir lime leaves to the pot. Bring to the boil. Add lime juice and mix well.

• Place a few dumplings in a soup bowl and ladle some coconut soup over. Serve hot.

From top: Steamed Soft Bean Curd with Thai Sauce, Dumplings and Vegetables in Coconut Milk Soup

BAKED MUSHROOM AND OLIVES

• PREPARATION TIME: 30 MIN • COOKING TIME: 30 MIN • SERVES 4

INGREDIENTS

Water	2.5 litres
Macaroni	180 g
Butter	25 g
Olive oil	2 Tbsp
Onion	1, cut into cubes
Garlic	2 cloves, chopped
Oregano leaves	2 tsp, chopped
Oyster mushrooms	300 g, each torn in half
Tomatoes	435 g, chopped
Tomato paste	1 Tbsp
Cashew nuts	60 g
Almonds	60 g
Salt to taste	
Olives	50 g, sliced
Freshly ground pepper	1 tsp
Cheddar cheese	125 g
Sesame seeds	60 g

METHOD

• Bring water to boil and cook macaroni until al dente according to package instructions. Drain and toss with butter. Set aside.

• Preheat oven to 180°C.

• Heat olive oil in a frying pan and sauté onion, garlic and oregano leaves for 2 minutes or until onions are soft. Add oyster mushrooms, tomatoes, tomato paste, cashew nuts, almonds and salt to taste. Stir well. Cook for 5 minutes, stirring constantly.

• Add olives and freshly ground pepper. Cook for 2 minutes. Transfer mixture to a greased ovenproof dish. Spoon in cooked buttered macaroni and sprinkle with cheese and sesame seeds.

• Bake for 20 minutes or until cheese is melted and golden brown. Serve hot.

MIXED BEAN SALAD

• PREPARATION TIME: 25 MIN • SERVES 6

INGREDIENTS

Red kidney beans	250 g, boiled
White kidney beans	180 g
Chickpeas	250 g, oiled
Mint leaves	4 Tbsp, chopped finely
Lemon rind	grated from 1 lemon

SALAD DRESSING

Lemon juice	1
Sugar	2 Tbsp
Salt	1 tsp
Ground white pepper	$1/2$ tsp
Garlic	3 cloves, chopped finely
Olive oil	90 ml

METHOD

• In a salad bowl, mix together both the red and white kidney beans, chick peas, mint leaves and lemon rind. Mix well.

• Combine ingredients for salad dressing and mix well. Add bean mixture and toss well. Chill in the fridge and serve cold.

CHEF'S NOTE

Pasta shapes may be added to make this salad even more substantial. Cook 180 g pasta shapes and toss with the other ingredients.

From left: Mixed Bean Salad, Baked Mushrooms and Olives

SPAGHETTI WITH VEGETARIAN NEAPOLITAN SAUCE

• PREPARATION TIME: 30 MIN • COOKING TIME: 30 MIN • SERVES 4

INGREDIENTS

Cooking oil	2 Tbsp
Garlic	8, chopped
Big onions	3, sliced
Tomato paste	1½ Tbsp
Chilli sauce	4 Tbsp
Ripe tomatoes	300 g, skinned and mashed
Oregano leaves	1½ tsp, chopped
Bay leaves	2
Basil leaves	2 sprigs, stems removed
Thyme	1 tsp
Sugar	1 Tbsp
Salt to taste	
Ground white pepper	1 tsp
Water	125 ml
Spaghetti	500 g, cooked
Parmesan cheese	125 g, grated

METHOD

• Heat oil and fry garlic until lightly browned and fragrant.

• Add onion slices, tomato paste, chilli sauce, ripe tomatoes, oregano leaves, bay leaves, basil leaves, thyme, sugar, salt and pepper. Mix well and stir in water. Cook until sauce is thick.

• Pour sauce over cooked spaghetti, sprinkle with Parmesan and serve.

PITA BREAD SUPREME PIZZA

• PREPARATION TIME: 30 MIN • COOKING TIME: 30 MIN • SERVES 4

INGREDIENTS

Cooking oil	1 Tbsp
Garlic	2 cloves, chopped
Onion	3, cut into cubes
Vegetarian mock chicken	250 g
Tomato paste	1½ Tbsp
Chilli sauce	4 Tbsp
Ripe tomatoes	300 g, skinned and mashed
Oregano leaves	1½ tsp, chopped
Bay leaves	2
Sugar	1 Tbsp
Salt to taste	
Ground white pepper	1 tsp
Pita bread	2
Mozzarella cheese	400 g, grated

METHOD

• Heat oil in a frying pan. Sauté garlic and onion cubes until soft. Add mock chicken and cook until lightly browned.

• Add tomato paste, chilli sauce, ripe tomatoes, oregano leaves, bay leaves, sugar, salt and pepper and stir. Continue to cook until sauce is thick.

• Place pita bread on a baking tray. Spread with some thick sauce and top with olives, mixed vegetables, pineapple cubes, capsicum slices and/or tomatoes.

• Sprinkle mozzarella over topping and bake in a preheated oven at 180°C until cheese is melted.

• Serve hot.

From Top: Spaghetti with Vegetarian Neapolitan Sauce, Pita Bread Supreme Pizza

LEEK AND TOMATO QUICHE

• PREPARATION TIME: 35 MIN • COOKING TIME: 45 MIN • SERVES 6

INGREDIENTS

Cottage cheese	125 g
Butter	75 g
Plain flour	200 g
Oil	1 Tbsp
Onion	1, sliced thinly
Leek	1 big stalk, cut into 2-cm lengths
Eggs	3, lightly beaten
Cream	180 g
Sun-dried tomatoes	60 g
Basil leaves	1 sprig
Parmesan cheese	60 g
Mozzarella cheese	125 g

METHOD

• Combine cottage cheese, butter and flour and mix into a dough. Knead gently on a floured surface until smooth. Cover and chill in the fridge for 20 minutes.

• Preheat oven to 190°C.

• Roll chilled dough into a sheet large enough to line a 20-cm round flan tin. Lay pastry over tin and pat it in neatly. Trim edges.

• Bake for 10 minutes or until light brown. Set aside.

• Heat oil and fry onion and leek until soft. Leave to drain on absorbent kitchen paper.

• Beat eggs and cream together. Set aside.

• When onions and leeks are sufficiently drained, place them evenly together with the sun-dried tomatoes, basil leaves and Parmesan cheese baked pastry case.

• Preheat oven to 190°C.

• Top with egg and cream mixture and sprinkle with mozzarella. Bake for 35 minutes until set. Let cool slightly, then cut into wedges to serve.

MINESTRONE SOUP WITH FRESH HERBS

• PREPARATION TIME: 30 MIN • COOKING TIME: 45 MIN • SERVES 6

INGREDIENTS

Cooking oil	2 Tbsp
Garlic	3 cloves, chopped
Potato	1, cut into small cubes
Celery	125 g, cut into small cubes
Cabbage	50 g, cut into small pieces
French beans	6, cut into small pieces
Leek	50 g, cut into small pieces
Bay leaves	2
Thyme	1/2 tsp
Parsley flakes	1 tsp
Vegetable stock	1.25 litres (refer to page 82)
Ground black pepper	1 tsp
Salt to taste	
Shell pasta	150 g, cooked

METHOD

• Heat oil in a pot and fry garlic until brown.

• Add cut vegetables, bay leaves, thyme, parsley flakes and vegetable stock. Bring to the boil and cook for 10 minutes.

• Add pepper and salt to taste. Add cooked pasta and serve hot.

From top: Leek and Tomato Quiche, Minestrone Soup with Fresh Herbs

MIXED VEGETABLES WITH HERB DIP

• PREPARATION TIME: 25 MIN • SERVES 4

INGREDIENTS

Broccoli	300 g, cut into florets
Cauliflower	300 g, cut into florets
Carrot	200 g, cut into 5-cm lengths
Button mushrooms	250 g
Potatoes	300 g, small, boiled and halved

HERB DIP

Fresh parsley	2 sprigs, chopped
Fresh basil	2 sprigs, chopped
Mayonnaise	125 ml
Sour cream	85 ml
Mustard	2 tsp
Freshly ground Black pepper	$1/2$ tsp
Sugar	1 Tbsp
Salt	1 tsp
Gherkins	2, chopped finely

METHOD

• Steam broccoli, cauliflower, carrot, mushrooms and potatoes until half done. Run over with cold water and set aside.

• Mix all herb dip ingredients together until well-blended.

• Serve with cut vegetables.

MIXED VEGETABLE CROQUETTES

• PREPARATION TIME: 35 MIN • COOKING TIME: 30 MIN • SERVES 4

INGREDIENTS

Cauliflower	300 g, cut into florets
Mixed vegetables	125 g
Egg	1, lightly beaten
Bran	4 Tbsp
Ricotta/Cottage cheese	4 Tbsp, grated
Parsley	2 sprigs, chopped
Chives	3 sprigs, chopped finely
Cheddar cheese	60 g, grated
Bread crumbs	50 g

METHOD

• Blanch cauliflower until very tender and drain.

• Mash cauliflower and mixed vegetables. Combine with egg, bran, ricotta or cottage cheese, parsley and chives. Mix well together.

• Preheat oven to 180°C.

• Shape mixture into balls. Coat with grated Cheddar and breadcrumbs.

• Place on a greased ovenproof dish and bake for 20 minutes or until brown. Serve hot with chilli or tomato sauce.

From top: Mixed Vegetables with Herb Dip, Mixed Vegetable Croquettes

SWEET CORN SOUP

• PREPARATION TIME: 30 MIN • COOKING TIME: 45 MIN • SERVES 4

INGREDIENTS

Vegetable stock	1.5 litres (*refer to page 82*)
Onion	1, cut into small cubes
Leek	1, white part only, cut into small pieces
Potatoes	3, cut into small cubes
Salt to taste	
Freshly ground pepper	1/2 tsp
Fresh milk	125 ml
Evaporated milk	125 ml
Canned sweet corn	250 g, blended finely
Parsley	2 sprigs, chopped finely

METHOD

• Bring vegetable stock to the boil in a stockpot. Add onion, leek and potatoes. Season with salt and pepper. Return stock to the boil, then lower heat, cover pot and simmer for 20 minutes.

• Remove vegetables from stock and blend into a fine purée using a blender. Return purée to the stock.

• Add fresh milk, evaporated milk, sweet corn and parsley, and mix well. Bring to the boil and cook for 5 minutes.

• Serve hot.

LASAGNE

• PREPARATION TIME: 30 MIN • COOKING TIME: 45 MIN • SERVES 6

INGREDIENTS

Long brinjal (aubergine/ eggplant)	1, large
Olive oil	1 Tbsp
Lemon juice	3 Tbsp
Onion	1, cut into small cubes
Garlic	2 cloves, chopped
Tomato juice	2 Tbsp
Canned tomatoes	440 g, peeled
Tomato purée	125 ml
Oregano leaves	2 tsp
Basil leaves	1 sprig, stems removed
Paprika	1/2 tsp
Lasagne sheets	8 sheets
Breadcrumbs	3 Tbsp
Cheddar cheese	185 g
Mozzarella cheese	125 g, grated

METHOD

• Cut brinjals in half lengthwise. Brush with olive oil and lemon juice and grill until soft. Set aside.

• Heat a non-stick pan and cook onions, garlic and tomato juice for 3 minutes until onions are soft. Add canned tomatoes, tomato purée, oregano leaves, basil leaves and paprika and stir well. Cook for 5 minutes.

• Spread a third of tomato mixture in an ovenproof dish and top with three lasagne sheets, half the quantity of breadcrumbs and some mozzarella cheese. Cover with a layer of brinjal and top with cheddar cheese. Repeat the process of layering and end with a layer of tomato mixture.

• Preheat oven to 180°C.

• Top with mozzarella cheese and bake for 45 minutes. Serve warm.

From top: Sweet Corn Soup, Lasagne

GRILLED MIXED VEGETABLE PIE

• PREPARATION TIME: 35 MIN • COOKING TIME: 40 MIN • SERVES 6

INGREDIENTS

Cooking oil	2 Tbsp
Garlic	2 cloves, chopped
Cabbage	150 g
Mixed vegetables	150 g
French beans	150 g
Red chilli	1, sliced
Cauliflower	150 g, cut into florets
Turmeric powder	1/2 tsp
Salt to taste	
Paprika	1/2 tsp
Water	4 Tbsp
Potatoes	500 g, boiled and mashed
Fresh milk	4 Tbsp
Butter	50 g
Ground black pepper	1/2 tsp
Cheddar cheese	125 g, grated
Sesame seeds	2 tsp

METHOD

• Heat oil in a wok and fry garlic until aromatic. Add cabbage, mixed vegetables, French beans, red chilli, cauliflower, turmeric powder, salt and paprika. Stir well.

• Add water, cover and cook until vegetables are half done. Transfer vegetables to an ovenproof dish and spread evenly. Set aside.

• Combine mashed potatoes with fresh milk, butter, salt and pepper and mix well.

• Preheat oven to 180°C.

• Spoon mashed potato mixture into a piping bag and pipe a basket weave pattern over vegetables ovenproof dish. Sprinkle with grated cheese and sesame seeds.

• Bake until top is golden brown. Serve hot.

FETTUCCINE WITH TOMATOES AND CHEESE SALAD

• PREPARATION TIME: 30 MIN • COOKING TIME: 25 MIN • SERVES 4

INGREDIENTS

Water	2.5 litres
Fettuccine	500 g
Butter	50 g
Olive oil	1 Tbsp
Garlic	2 cloves, chopped
Onions	2, chopped
Tomato purée	250 ml
Basil leaves	2 sprigs, chopped finely
Parsley	2 sprigs, chopped finely
Oregano leaves	1 tsp
Tomatoes	2, skinned, seeded and cut into cubes
Salt to taste	
Parmesan cheese	100 g, grated

METHOD

• Bring water to the boil and cook fettuccine according to package instructions. When ready, rinse under cold water. Drain and toss with butter. Set aside.

• In a salad bowl, combine olive oil, garlic, onions, tomato purée, basil leaves, parsley, oregano, tomatoes, salt and cooked fettuccine. Toss well.

• Chill in the fridge for 2–3 hours. Serve cold, sprinkled with Parmesan cheese.

From top: Grilled Mixed Vegetable Pie, Fettuccine with Tomatoes and Cheese Salad

VEGETABLE BURGERS

• PREPARATION TIME: 35 MIN • COOKING TIME: 30 MIN • SERVES 4

INGREDIENTS

Button mushrooms	125 g
Broccoli	500 g, cut into florets
Courgette (zucchini)	500 g, chopped
Carrots	25 g, chopped
Big onions	2, chopped
Garlic	3 cloves, chopped
Parsley leaves	2 sprigs, chopped
Breadcrumbs	185 g
Plain flour	125 g
Egg	1, lightly beaten
Salt to taste	
Ground black pepper	1 tsp
Burger buns	6, sliced
Cooking oil	125 ml
Lettuce leaves	200 g, torn into medium-sized pieces

HERB TOMATO SAUCE

Olive oil	1 Tbsp
Big onion	1, chopped finely
Garlic	2, chopped finely
Red chilli	1, seeds removed and chopped finely
Green chilli	1, seeds removed and chopped finely
Canned stewed tomatoes	440 g, mashed finely

METHOD

• Blanch button mushrooms, broccoli, courgette and carrots separately, then place in a food processor with onions, garlic and parsley. Blend into a fine purée.

• Transfer purée to a bowl and add breadcrumbs, flour, egg, salt and powder. Knead into a firm dough. Cover and refrigerate for 30 minutes.

• Remove chilled dough from fridge and form into patties.

• Heat oil and fry patties on both sides until lightly brown. Set aside.

• To make sauce, heat olive oil and sauté onions, garlic, red and green chillies until soft. Add stewed tomatoes and bring to the boil. Leave to simmer for 5 minutes to reduce stock.

• Place a lettuce leaf, a spoonful of tomato sauce and a fried vegetable patty in each burger bun. Serve immediately.

POTATO AND BRINJAL GRATIN

• PREPARATION TIME: 20 MIN • COOKING TIME: 35 MIN • SERVES 6

INGREDIENTS

Potatoes	250 g, boiled and sliced
Brinjals (aubergine/ eggplant)	250 g, sliced thinly
Garlic	2 cloves, chopped
Double cream	250 ml
Salt to taste	
Ground black pepper	$1/2$ tsp
Basil leaves	1 sprig, chopped finely
Garlic cheese	100 g, grated
Mozzarella cheese	15 g, grated
Butter	30 g

METHOD

• Preheat oven to 200°C.

• Arrange potato and brinjal slices in a greased ovenproof dish. Set aside.

• In a bowl, mix garlic with double cream, salt and pepper.

• Stir in basil leaves and mix well. Pour mixture over sliced vegetables. Sprinkle with grated cheese and dot with butter.

• Bake 20-25 minutes until golden brown. Serve hot.

Anti-clockwise From Top: Vegetable Burger, Potato and Brinjal Gratin, Herb Tomato Sauce

GLOSSARY OF INGREDIENTS

Basil
Asian basil or sweet basil is widely used in Thailand. Basil leaves are used fresh as they do not retain their flavour when dried.

Torch Ginger Flower
For culinary purposes, the torch ginger flower is picked when still in bud form. It can be eaten raw or cooked. It is commonly added to curries and some salads.

Banana Flower
Also known as banana heart, it is found at the end of the banana fruit bunch. The tough outer layers must be removed until the yellow part is exposed. This part may be finely cubed and cooked with spices or blanched and eaten with sauce dip.

Kaffir Lime Leaf
Kaffir lime leaves may be eaten raw or cooked. They are commonly used to flavour salads, curries and soups.

Curry Leaves
Curry leaves have a distinctive fragrance and the flavour is greatly enhanced when the leaves are fried. Each sprig may contain 12-16 small leaves.

Young Jackfruit
The jackfruit has a hard rind with bumpy spikes. It changes from green to yellowish when mature. The flesh and seeds of young jackfruit are edible and can be used in curries and salads.

Lesser Ginger
Lesser ginger or *krachai* as it is known in Thai, comes in bunches of slender, short tuberous roots. They are brown in colour and have a mild flavour. They may be omitted if unavailable.

Oyster Mushrooms
Oyster mushrooms are eaten fresh. The young variety of these fan-shaped mushrooms is considered the best.

Chinese Chives
Also known as *ku chai* and garlic chives, Chinese chives have thick, long, flat leaves like the spring onion (scallion) and a stronger flavour than the Western chives. It is used both as a herb and vegetable in Southeast Asian cooking.

Galangal
A member of the ginger family, galangal is also known as greater galangal to distinguish it from another variety from China, known as lesser galangal. Preferably used fresh, galangal is also available in dried and powdered form.

Wood Ear Fungus
Wood ear fungus is a mild-flavoured mushroom. When reconstituted, it expands five to six times in size and has a crunchy consistency.

Bengal
Gram Dhal

Dhal
Dhal are dried pulses and there are almost 60 varieties available in India, including lentils, peas and mung beans.

Gram Dhal

Tamarind
The tamarind fruit is commonly used in Southeast Asian cooking. The pods contain pulp-covered seeds, which is soaked in water for 7–10 minutes, then strained of any fibres and seeds to obtain the sour juice.

81

BASIC RECIPES

BOILED COCONUT CREAM
PREPARATION TIME: 5 MIN • COOKING TIME: 20 MIN
• MAKES 1 PORTION

Grated coconut	500 g
Water	435 ml

- Combine grated coconut and water.
  Squeeze and extract coconut milk.
- Boil coconut milk until it separates
  and milk to reduced to 250 ml.

THICK AND THIN COCONUT MILK
PREPARATION TIME: 10 MIN • MAKES 1 PORTION

Grated coconut	500 g
Water	680 ml

- Combine grated coconut and 180 ml water.
  Squeeze to extract 250 ml thick coconut milk.
- Add 500 ml water to the grated coconut and
  extract thin coconut milk.

VEGETABLE STOCK
PREPARATION TIME: 10 MIN • COOKING TIME: 2 HR
• MAKES 1 PORTION

Carrots	540 g, sliced
Celery	200 g, sliced
Long beans	200 g, sliced
French beans	200 g, sliced
Tomatoes	2
Water	2.5 litres

- Combine ingredients in a stockpot
  and boil for 2 hours over a slow fire.
  Strain and refrigerate.

VEGETARIAN CURRY PASTE
PREPARATION TIME: 10 MIN • COOKING TIME: 20 MIN
• MAKES 1 PORTION

Fresh red chillies	200 g
Dried chillies	50 g, soaked in hot water
Candle nuts	100 g
Coriander seeds	60 g
Fresh turmeric	20 g
Lemongrass (*serai*)	4 stalks
Salt	2 Tbsp
Brown sugar	60 g
Cooking oil	90 ml

- Grind all ingredients except oil together until fine.
- Heat oil and fry ground ingredients until oil rises to the
  top. Let cool. Store in an airtight container in the fridge
  until needed.

AMTI MASALA POWDER
PREPARATION TIME: 10 MIN • COOKING TIME: 10 • MAKES 1 PORTION

Cooking oil	1 Tbsp
Coriander seeds	100 g
Dry chillies	100 g
Sesame seeds	4 Tbsp, toasted
Cumin seeds	2 Tbsp
Black pepper	2 Tbsp
Cinnamon	3 sticks
Cloves	2
Bay leaves	6
Caraway seeds	2 tsp
Asafoetida	1 tsp
Turmeric powder	3 Tbsp
Rock salt	1 Tbsp

• Heat oil in a pan and fry ingredients until aromatic.
• Pour into a blender and blend until fine. Store in an airtight container until needed.

HOT CHILLI PASTE
PREPARATION TIME: 10 MIN • COOKING TIME: 30 MIN • MAKES 1 PORTION

Dried chillies	150 g

• Soak chillies in hot water for 30 minutes.
• Drain and grind into a fine paste.
• Add salt to taste.

GARAM MASALA
PREPARATION TIME: 2 HR • COOKING TIME: 10 MIN • MAKES 1 PORTION

Cumin seeds	240 g
Black peppercorns	60 g
Cinnamon	60 g, broken into small pieces
Cloves	60 g
Black cardamoms	120 g

• Rinse ingredients and sun-dry.
• Dry-fry for 5 minutes and grind until fine.
• Store in an airtight container until needed.

Note: Ready-made garam masala is available from specialty stores and Indian grocery shops.

SAMBAR POWDER
PREPARATION TIME: 10 MIN • COOKING TIME: 15 MIN • MAKES 1 PORTION

Coriander seeds	6 tsp
Dried red chillies	24
Gram dhal	90 g
Fenugreek seeds	3 tsp
Black peppercorns	45 g
Mustard seeds	45 g

• Dry-fry ingredients and grind until fine.
• Store in an airtight container until needed.

WEIGHTS & MEASURES

Quantities for this book are given in Metric and American (spoon and cup) measures. Standard spoon and cup measurements used are: 1 teaspoon = 5 ml, 1 dessertspoon = 10 ml, 1 tablespoon = 15 ml, 1 cup = 250 ml. All measures are level unless otherwise stated.

LIQUID AND VOLUME MEASURES

Metric	Imperial	American
5 ml	$\frac{1}{6}$ fl oz	1 teaspoon
10 ml	$\frac{1}{3}$ fl oz	1 dessertspoon
15 ml	$\frac{1}{2}$ fl oz	1 tablespoon
60 ml	2 fl oz	$\frac{1}{4}$ cup (4 tablespoons)
85 ml	$2\frac{1}{2}$ fl oz	$\frac{1}{3}$ cup
90 ml	3 fl oz	$\frac{3}{8}$ cup (6 tablespoons)
125 ml	4 fl oz	$\frac{1}{2}$ cup
180 ml	6 fl oz	$\frac{3}{4}$ cup
250 ml	8 fl oz	1 cup
300 ml	10 fl oz ($\frac{1}{2}$ pint)	$1\frac{1}{4}$ cups
375 ml	12 fl oz	$1\frac{1}{2}$ cups
435 ml	14 fl oz	$1\frac{3}{4}$ cups
500 ml	16 fl oz	2 cups
625 ml	20 fl oz (1 pint)	$2\frac{1}{2}$ cups
750 ml	24 fl oz ($1\frac{1}{5}$ pints)	3 cups
1 litre	32 fl oz ($1\frac{3}{5}$ pints)	4 cups
1.25 litres	40 fl oz (2 pints)	5 cups
1.5 litres	48 fl oz ($2\frac{2}{5}$ pints)	6 cups
2.5 litres	80 fl oz (4 pints)	10 cups

DRY MEASURES

Metric	Imperial
30 grams	1 ounce
45 grams	$1\frac{1}{2}$ ounces
55 grams	2 ounces
70 grams	$2\frac{1}{2}$ ounces
85 grams	3 ounces
100 grams	$3\frac{1}{2}$ ounces
110 grams	4 ounces
125 grams	$4\frac{1}{2}$ ounces
140 grams	5 ounces
280 grams	10 ounces
450 grams	16 ounces (1 pound)
500 grams	1 pound, $1\frac{1}{2}$ ounces
700 grams	$1\frac{1}{2}$ pounds
800 grams	$1\frac{3}{4}$ pounds
1 kilogram	2 pounds, 3 ounces
1.5 kilograms	3 pounds, $4\frac{1}{2}$ ounces
2 kilograms	4 pounds, 6 ounces

LENGTH

Metric	Imperial
0.5 cm	$\frac{1}{4}$ inch
1 cm	$\frac{1}{2}$ inch
1.5 cm	$\frac{3}{4}$ inch
2.5 cm	1 inch

OVEN TEMPERATURE

Regulo	°C	°F	Gas
Very slow	120	250	1
Slow	150	300	2
Moderately slow	160	325	3
Moderate	180	350	4
Moderately hot	190/200	370/400	5/6
Hot	210/220	410/440	6/7
Very hot	230	450	8
Super hot	250/290	475/550	9/10